ProfitSourcing.com

MW00931594

Book Flipping

10 Steps to Setting up and Fully Automating a Used Book Selling Business on Amazon

By Bryan Young
www.profitsourcing.com

ProfitSourcing.com

To Bob (Dad),
without your lifetime of encouragement
none of this would have been possible.
Thank you!

BOOK FLIPPING
Published by Bryan R Young
203 Lyman Ct NE Suite #1
Racine, MN 55967

Cover Designed by
Alinda Velist
(https://www.fiverr.com/alindavelist)

© 2015 Bryan Young
Published by YoungLife Publishing Company

Earnings Disclaimer
I can't make any promises as to how much money you'll make following
this book-selling system. It's completely up to you to take what's learned
here and to accurately apply it to an online business. I can't promise you
that you'll make money, in fact you could lose money on the business
ventures suggested in this book. But, I'm here to help you avoid that.

I suggest finding a local Certified Public Accountant (CPA) that can help
give you professional financial direction.

ProfitSourcing.com
Table of Contents

Bonus Video!

How much money do you want to make selling used books? $1,000 per week in net profit? $2,000 per week? In this free video I will share with you how much inventory you will need to have in stock to anticipate that sort of income (according to my sales figures).

As a big "Thank You" for buying this book check out this free video!

To access this free 15 minute video on "Knowing Your Numbers" go to: https://profitsourcing.leadpages.co/thankyou/

Introduction

"Your time is limited, so don't waste it living someone else's life. Don't be trapped by dogma, which is living with the results of other people's thinking. Don't let the noise of other's opinions drown out your inner voice. And most importantly, have courage to follow your heart and intuition. They somehow already know what you truly want to become. Everything else is secondary."
-Steve Jobs

"I don't know the key to success, but the key to failure is trying to please everybody."
-Bill Cosby

Selling on Amazon

Have you ever thought about making some serious money selling physical products on Amazon? Did you know that in less than two years, with a little hustle and gumption your home-based online selling business could be bringing in as much as 6-figures in annual income? Maybe, you understand the possibilities that are out there in the online selling world, but have you explored the opportunities that are there in the used book selling market? Understanding that the profit margin on used, physical books, is astronomical and we'll discuss more on this soon. What if I told you that there is a way for you to not only make excellent money selling books on Amazon but also to outsource the whole operation? With the proven business model that I've developed and deployed, you can reap all of the benefits of running a profitable online book selling business without having to do any of the work yourself.

The buying, prepping, shipping, re-pricing, customer service and overall management of the book-selling arm of our online selling company has been fully outsourced. In this 10 Step Guide, I pull back the curtain on our book-selling business model. Because I want to inspire you and help you achieve some of the same success that I've attained online, I'm willing to bare it all. In the following chapters, I'll share with you all of my sourcing strategies and criteria. Not only will I share with you general outsourcing philosophy, I'll show you exactly, step-by-step, how I am applying it. I'll even be transparent with our earnings so that you can see the full potential of this online business.

We have in no way, shape or form achieved the maximum level of profitability for our book-selling business. We still make mistakes, and we are still learning along the way but we've come a long way. A great way to learn a new business model, without having to make all of the mistakes yourself, is to learn from the mistakes of others. Learn from my mistakes. Apply the strategies that have a proven track record of success and avoid the pitfalls. As we continue to scale this business into uncharted territory, I'll continue to share with you what we are learning along the way!

Who is this book for?

This book is for anyone who would like to start their own book selling business. If you'd like to get into the used media selling market but don't know where to start, this book will lay it all out for you even if you're not ready to outsource yet. Maybe you'd like to just do some book selling online yourself, before you even consider expanding, that's fine. And, with this book you'll able to provide for yourself a great foundation for success.

I know many online sellers who are proud to be a team of "One", they do all of the book sourcing, prepping, and shipping, themselves and they make a nice yearly income. They maintain complete control of their business, and don't need to worry themselves with the additional challenges that come when managing people. In the pages of this book, you'll find all of the information necessary to get set up with the best equipment, establish a solid book-buying criteria, strategize your local and national book selling geography, and will be given ways to expand your entrepreneurial mind.

But, I want to warn you "self-employed" minded friends I'm going to be trying to instill within you an outsourcing mindset along the way. Hopefully by the end of the book, whether you decided to follow suit or not, I will have laid out a compelling argument for turning your active selling, book-selling business into a passive stream of income.

If your desire from the get-go is to start and as quickly as possible, outsource your online used book selling business then you'll be very happy with this read. From what I lay out in the subsequent chapters, you'll be able to start your own thriving passive online book selling business from start to finish. Not only will you benefit from the tools and sourcing strategies that I share but you'll also benefit from advice on how to compensate your workers, and how to provide a foundation of success for those who source, ship and help manage your company. I'll discuss the importance of hiring top-talent and the best way to build a high functioning, online selling team. This 10 Step Plan, plus the free online resources will give you everything that you need to get this business model up and running.

For those of you who have no desire for selling used books, I still feel like there is some value for you to be gained from learning from my experiences, especially if you have an online or offline business and you are interested in hiring people. You are probably looking for ways to expand and outsource some of the tasks in your business and my hope is that this behind-the-curtain look at our book selling business will be sort of an inspiration to you. Outsourcing does work, and if neglected I'm afraid that you and your business may be missing out on some great scaling opportunities.

About Me

Before we jump right into the content, I wanted to tell you a little bit about me. I'm married to a wonderful woman, Chelsea, and together we have six kids. Yeah, I said SIX and that wasn't a typo, and yes we are well aware how the whole pregnancy thing comes about. Just to clear things up, our kids are 2 to 12 years old and we have three of each. We live in SE Minnesota.

In 2012, I discovered the possibilities of selling on Amazon. I already had some part-time experience selling online, mainly on eBay, but with the advent of all of the new possibilities that there were for little sellers, such as me, on Amazon with F.B.A. (more on this in Step #2), I quickly made the switch. In 2013, I quit my job in nursing at the Mayo Clinic to be a stay-at-home Dad and part time online business man. Our "Why" for starting and working so hard on building our online business was not the money, power, or prestige, but it was the opportunity to maximize our time with the people that we love most, our family.

Working full-time meant that my attention was divided and that I was missing out on a lot of the childhood milestones that I didn't want to miss out on. Also, Chelsea's my best friend and the thought of being able to spend time with her, working side-by-side on a home-based business, was very appealing. In 2013, we did just under $100k in sales, so in January 2014 Chelsea left her very secure, high-paying job in X-ray, also at the Mayo Clinic, so that we could both pursue online selling full-time.

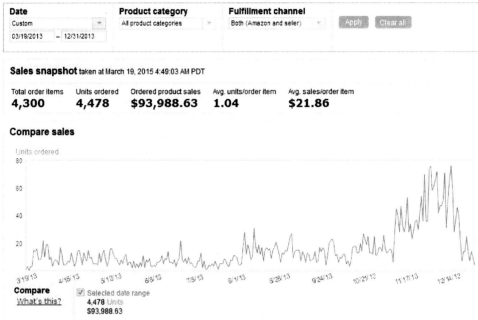

Figure 1

Here are our Amazon sales for the year of 2013(Figure 1):

In 2013, while spending serious time managing the household, I was able to sell 4,478 items at an average price of $21.86 per item. And, as you can see from the graph, the Amazon data only goes back as far as Mid-March (although we had sales in the first few months of the year). Here's a breakdown of the categories that we were selling in at the time (Figure 2):

Product category	Ordered product sales	% of ordered product sales	
Toys	$123,450.96	41.75%	
Books	$36,336.47	12.29%	
Kitchen	$28,367.36	9.59%	
Grocery	$22,771.81	7.70%	
Home Appliances	$10,268.36	3.47%	
All other categories	$74,478.74	25.19%	

Figure 2

Toys in 2013 dominated, and they still dominate our sales to this day. There's something about selling toys online that's fun. Maybe it's the nostalgia factor, or that we are very kid-oriented. I guess it could be that there's a decent profit to be made in that category. But as you can see our second best category for the year was Books. Now, keep in mind all of the books we sold in 2013 and most of 2014 were sourced and shipped by us. We didn't hire people to buy books for us until the end of Q3 in 2014.

2014 was a great year, and with Chelsea and I both home full time we were able to dedicate some serious effort to the online business. Not only did we hit the ground running but we had fun along the way. We made lots of costly sourcing mistakes but none of them were major, and we learned from them all. Here's our numbers for 2014 (Figure 3):

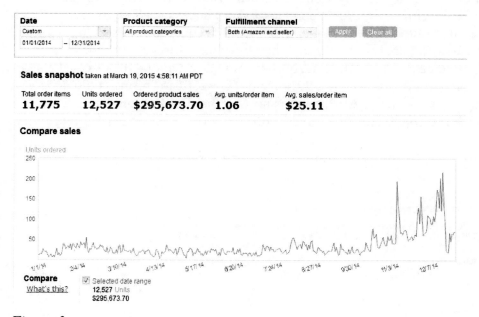

Figure 3

Our sales in 2014, as a result of our added hustle and online selling experience more than tripled. This year we sold over 12,500 items at an even higher ASP (Average Sale Price). If you are having a hard time visualizing what 12,500 items looks like, we sold 34 items per day, on average, from January to the end of December. You may have noticed the huge spike in sales in both 2013 and 2014 in Q4. For most online sellers and retailers, Q4 is the most profitable time of the year. Here's the category breakdown for 2014 (Figure 4):

Product category	Ordered product sales	% of ordered product sales	
Toys	$123,450.96	41.75%	
Books	$36,336.47	12.29%	
Kitchen	$28,367.36	9.59%	
Grocery	$22,771.81	7.70%	
Home Appliances	$10,268.36	3.47%	
All other categories	$74,478.74	25.19%	

Figure 4

The Toy category still commands the lead at 41.75% of ordered product sales and the top five is rounded off with Books (12.29%), Kitchen (9.59%), Grocery (7.70%) and Home Appliances (3.47%). In July of 2014 we hired our first Book-Sourcer, someone who we would pay to go to thrift-stores, analyze books and then buy them. Already our books, as a percentage of all of our Amazon sales was down about 10% from the year before (from 22.02% to 12.29%), and if it wasn't for hiring some people to buy books for us in 2014, there is no way that Books would have even made the Top 5. Here's some data on just book sales for 2014 (Figure 5):

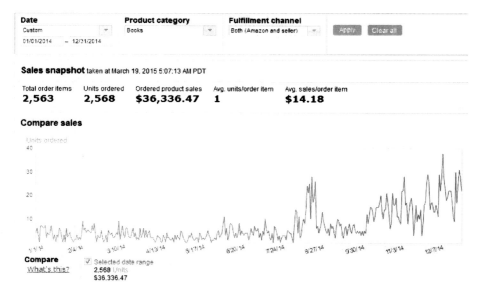

Figure 5

Did you notice the huge spike in sales in July? That was all thanks to our new Book Sourcer & Manager (more on him in Step #8 Hire Top Talent). Due to the time-consuming nature of book sourcing and shipping, and more importantly due to all of the success and fun we were having in other Amazon categories, we would have stopped sourcing and selling books all together, if it wasn't for this move. We knew that there was tons of profit to be made selling used books, but we just didn't have the time to do it. If we hadn't explored the option of outsourcing, our business would have really missed out.

So far this year (2015), this is where we are (Figure 6):

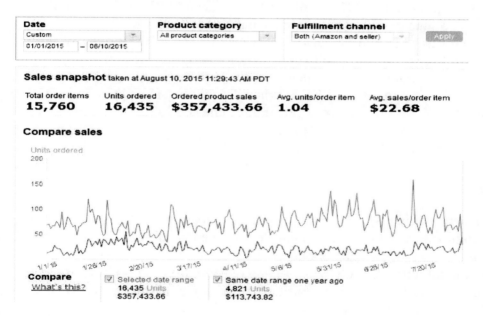

Figure 6

We're only part way through Q3 and we already have $357,433.66 in sales, earned from 16,435 units sold. This means that, on average we are selling more than 77 items per day, or 3.21 items per hour, which is great! But, you may be wondering, "How are book sales so far this year?" (Figure 7):

Product category	Ordered product sales	% of ordered product sales	
Books	$98,407.94	27.53%	▬
Toys	$60,921.03	17.04%	▬
Kitchen	$31,856.38	8.91%	▪
Shoes	$21,688.43	6.07%	▪
Clothing	$19,871.92	5.56%	▪
All other categories	$124,687.96	34.88%	▬▬

Figure 7

The Book category takes the lead, accounting for 27.53% of sales, Toys comes in second (17.04%) followed by Kitchen (8.91%), Shoes (6.07%) and Clothing (5.56%). There are a couple of reasons why Books did so well for us so far into 2015. 1) January is one of the best months of the year to sell books, especially non-fiction, due to the beginning of the second semester at many colleges throughout the country and that people generally stay in and read books when it's cold outside. Our worst months for used, non-fiction book selling are in June and July, when schools are out and the weather's nice. 2) In the beginning of 2014, we started moving away from the Toy category and into Clothing and Shoes. As we diversified our inventory a bit, Books had the opportunity to grasp that top spot.

The crazy thing is, we are in the process of scaling and out-sourcing our Retail Arbitrage business and have really been hustling. Retail Arbitrage is buying items, other than books, at local retail stores and selling them online for a profit. With this jolt in retail sourcing, I would have assumed that even with this new diversification, we would easily be able to outsell Books in our other categories, but obviously I was wrong!

This $98K in sales was all completely outsourced. The income that we derive from it is 99% passive, and in just a bit we'll define passive income, suffice to say passive income is typically never truly 100% passive, and we do what we can occasionally to keep the book-selling plates spinning. But, of the 7,427 books that we've sold over the last seven and ½ months, we haven't seen any of them. We didn't source, prepare, or ship them, all we have had to do is sit back and watch the sales come in! We took an extended 2 week vacation in February with the family to Disney world for

5 days and an eight night Southern Caribbean cruise. It felt great to get away and spend some time forming memories and having fun with the family. Whether we were snorkeling in Grand Turk, touring historical sites in Old San Juan, Hiking in St. Martin, or trying to remember to stay on the left side of the road in St. Thomas we didn't need to worry about the business.

Not only did the book business keep running, but it grew in profitability. I've been selling goods online for years and typically had to completely shut down my selling account when I went out of town, it felt great to have been able to set this business up and then watch it perpetuate itself, without my necessary involvement.

"What's Your Net Profit?"

You may be saying to yourself, "Well, Mr. Young $98k in sales sounds great, but what's the net profit on those books?" That's a great question. Here's a quick breakdown of our estimated sales figures. This is a "high-level" view of the profitability of our book selling company.

Here's the breakdown:
7,427 books sold (January through mid August 2015)
$98,407.94 in Gross Sales
$13.26 Average Sale Price per book

Expenses:
$3.75/book Cost to acquire a book ($1.50/book and $1.50 Finding and Listing fees), less Amazon fees
$5.25/book Amazon Fees

Profit:
$4.26/book profit
$31,639.02 total profit so far this year

Current inventory:
17,000 books for sale

I hope that you find this snap-shot encouraging. I just want you to be able to fully wrap your mind around the possibilities that are there in the world of book-selling. Although, we continue to expand our business and are reinvesting a good portion of the profits back into new inventory, $31,639.02 in 7 & ½ months is not too shabby! We will eventually reach an equilibrium point in which instead of growing our inventory we will just be maintaining it, and then we will be able to pocket most of the profits.

At our current pace we are bringing in over $4,200 per month in passive income! If we sustained these numbers for the whole year, we would bring in just over $50,000 annually. I hope that you see all of the potential in online selling!

Are you getting excited about book-selling? Are your eyes opened to the possibilities that are online selling? If so keep reading!

What exactly is Passive Income?

Passive income is earnings an individual makes from an enterprise in which he or she is not actively involved. It is money that is made with none or very little effort to maintain it. Passive or residual income is usually referred to as a "stream", once it has been established it will flow nearly independently. Once the initial investment has been made the earnings are irresistible. But, don't be misled by the name "passive", because this type of income requires a lot of active, upfront effort and resources.

It takes time and hard work to set up a stream of income that will provide you with some decent hands-off income. But, as I hope that you will soon realize, the end result is worth all of the work in the beginning. Some examples of passive income may include: income earned from a rental property, interest from a bank account, royalties earned from a published book or from licensing a patent, earnings from internet advertisements on websites, dividend and internet income. You may be wondering, "Is it hard to set up a passive income stream?"

Setting Up a Stream of Passive Income

The good news is, setting up a stream of passive income can be relatively cheap and easy, and it is a business model that can be implemented "on the side" for extra income in addition to your 9 to 5 job. Also, if start-up funds are a little tight, there are ways to start these types of business with little upfront investment and then you can just roll profits earned directly back into the business. The great thing about selling new and used books on Amazon is that they are very inexpensive to acquire. Low cost inventory and sky-high profit margins partner together for a winning combination (more on this to come).

Geographical Location is Not Important

Thanks to ever advancing technology, passive streams of income can be built and maintained from anywhere around the world. As I mentioned before, my family and I just got back from a extraordinary, fourteen day, vacation in the Southern Caribbean and Florida. During this time not only did our Amazon selling business do well, it continued to grow while providing us a very nice source of income.

Why Passive Income?

There are a number of reasons why you should consider adding some passive income streams to your portfolio. They allow you to make money anytime of the day, and once you get going, you can easily find ways to duplicate your results in other markets or areas and create multiple streams of passive income. Most importantly, if all goes well, you will have the freedom and flexibility to do whatever you want. For me, it is spending time with my wife and kids. My "why" is my family and a "win" for me is being able to spend a maximum amount of time with the people I love the most while I still have the chance. Building business systems that provide perpetual profit will give you the power to do what you want with your time.

Book-Selling

In the last 365 days, we have done $123,988.06 in books sales on Amazon. This gross sales figure represents 9,290 books sold at an average price of $13.35 each. That's more than 25 books a day, which means that we have been selling books at the rate of one book+ per hour! Here's the best part.

Due to the business system that we have in place, all of the training, sourcing, prepping, labeling, shipping and re-pricing has been completely outsourced. Which means that all of the income earned on our books sales over the last four months is completely residual.

We didn't do any work to acquire, sell and ship this inventory. Zero. Zip. And get this, not only has the sourcing, shipping, fulfillment and re-pricing been automated, Amazon will also handle any customer inquiries, refunds and returns. This has given us so much freedom!

Creating Passive income while leveraging Amazon FBA

Honestly, when most people think of selling on Amazon they think of lots and lots of hard work. First you need to find some profitable items to sell. Next, you need to list them on Amazon, and sometimes pictures and descriptions are required. Whether you ship them directly to the customer (Merchant Fulfillment) or to Amazon for fulfillment (FBA), there's lots prepping and shipping to do. Finally, once the customer receives the item, you still need to be on standby, just in case something goes wrong and you need to bust out some superior customer service.

Now, don't get me wrong. With a serious, well thought through system, you can run a very profitable Amazon business by doing all of this yourself, or as a family team. But, have you considered the alternatives? Can you build a solid passive income with Amazon?

Don't Be Indispensable

I know many successful online sellers who are having difficulty with the notion of outsourcing something that they believe would be impossible for someone else to do at the same level of success, or better. They've created an impressive business that would be impossible for them to step out of, because they have become the indispensable "Linchpin" in their own organization. In Seth Godin's book, *Linchpin: Are You Indispensable?* Godin lays out the compelling reasons why you should not be a replaceable cog in someone's business machine, but instead you should position yourself in a way that you become irreplaceable in the company. Be the employee that the company can't live without! Well, this is great for employees, but not entrepreneurs and not for business builders.

If you want to build a company that is truly excellent, it has to be bigger than yourself, and it can't depend on you in every aspect of its operations. It just can't. In fact if you really want to take your company to the next level you need to hire people that are smarter and better than you. That's right, find people that are superior at what they do. Find people that can complement your strengths and fill in gaps in areas that you are weak.

Let's Get At It!

These 10 Steps will help give you the guidance necessary to apply my success in online selling to your business. If this book encourages you to start your own book selling business so that you can 1) make some great profit, 2) provide good paying jobs for your friends and family, and 3) provide a very valuable service to Amazon customers throughout the world, great! But, if you decide not to sell books, don't fret on using the principles that I have applied in our book-selling business I'm confident they will prove helpful for you in whatever area of business you currently operate and are looking to expand. Sit back, relax, and let's hit the books!

Why Used Books?

"A pessimist sees the difficulty in every opportunity; an optimist sees the opportunity in every difficulty."
Winston S. Churchill

"Not knowing when the dawn will come I open every door."
Emily Dickinson

There's Opportunity on Every Shelf

You may be asking yourself, "Why books and not one of the other more popular, and more glamorous Amazon categories?" Great question.

Believe it or not, there are still some very nice profits to be made selling physical copies of books. With the creation of E-readers and the ability to read books on the computer or on other portable electronic devices, we have definitely seen a decline in the number of paperback and hardcover books sold, but print books are still in the lead. According to an article by Publishers Weekly, eBooks are still being outsold by hardcover and paperback:

"E-book sales accounted for 23% of unit sales in the first six months of 2014, according to Nielsen Books and Consumer's latest survey of the nation's book-buying behavior. Paperbacks remained the most popular format in the first half of the year, with a 42% share of unit sales. Hardcover's share of units was just ahead of eBooks, accounting for 25% of unit purchases."

What book categories have been affected most by the advent of eBooks? According to the same article, adult and young adult fiction within the trade book category. Other categories that have had some sales diverted to the E-format include children's and romance books. The important theme that I want you to notice here is that the Non-fiction category has not been mentioned. At least for the time being, and into the foreseeable future, people prefer to have physical copies of non-fiction books.

It's much easier to pull a book off of the shelf and page through it, looking for notes in the margins or underlining, to address a question I may have with a physical copy of a book than with an electronic version. Some day reference books may become more user friendly in this regard, but they're not there yet!

I wanted to quote Dale Carnegie in response to a Facebook post I saw yesterday, and since I had just read the book, I remembered that the

particular quote was about halfway through on the right hand side of the page distinguished by some underlining and a star. Finding that same quote on my Kindle, tablet, Smartphone or computer wouldn't have been as quick and easy.

In fact, while writing this book, I have pulled over a dozen books on business off of my shelf for inspiration and guidance. Often times I'm not entirely sure what I'm looking for, I just flip through relevant sections looking for anything that stands out. This research, at least in my opinion, would be markedly more difficult using eBooks.

I understand that this may all change in the future. I'm sure that technology will make it easier to use eBooks as reference books, but for the time being there are nice profits to be made in the non-fiction book selling business.

Amazon Wrote the Book on Used Book Selling

When Amazon burst onto the international scene, it was known as "the biggest bookstore on earth." Amazon sells over 100 million books per year. This figure represents over $7.96 billion in revenue per year! To put that in perspective, their closest book selling competitor, Barnes and Noble, only sells about $4.36 billion per year. While Amazon has expanded to a number of categories and has now become "The Everything Store", Barnes and Noble is trending in the other direction.

Everyone is shopping online, and all numbers indicate that online sales will only get better over the next decade. So the question isn't, "Should I be selling stuff online?" It should instead be, "How could I let an opportunity like this pass me buy?"

Next order of business is to find inventory, but don't dismay. Technology is on our side!

Let's Talk Profit

The profit margins in the used book selling business are crazy. Let's compare. Typically online sellers hope to find products that they can sell for a 60-100% ROI (Return on Investment). This means that for every dollar they spend on a particular item they would like to realize a net profit of somewhere between $.60 to $1.00. That's not a bad return right? I mean, if you asked Warren Buffet, the world famous investor, what ROI is a good ROI he would tell you is 20% annually. So, if you can get 60-100% consistently that's pretty solid.

With books it's different. On average, books at thrift-stores, library sales, rummage sales, garage sales, etc... can be sourced for about a dollar a piece. If we were to average out all of the additional expenses that are necessary to run this business we would probably need to tack on an additional $.25 per book (and that's a pretty liberal estimation). We currently have an average sale price (ASP) per book sold just of under $15. So assuming that Amazon will take about a third of the sale price in fees, we sell 100% FBA or Fulfillment by Amazon (I'll get into that later), that would leave us with a $8.75 net profit per book sold. Even if you're not a mathematician you can probably already begin to see how profitable this business is. If my total COGS (Cost of Goods Sold) is $1.25 and I plan to net $8.75 after all is said and done my ROI is 700%!

When considering whether or not a business is "outsource-able" you need to scrutinize financial measurements such as profit margin and ROI. When looking for outsourcing opportunities, you need to have a decent "Profit Cushion"(I made that phrase up), so that if you were to pay someone to do some, or all of the work for you (which would increase your COGS), you would still have some profits left over. Is there enough "Profit Cushion" in Retail or Online arbitrage, considering that you will have a 60-100% ROI? Yes, but with the ROI in used book-selling we see far greater potential. The cushion is so over-stuffed that you can afford to pay your people really good money for their work (I highly recommend this.) and still realize some tidy profits. I'll get into what I pay my book manager, book sourcing, and shipping people in a following chapter.

I am a firm advocate in creating business systems so that you can outsource all divisions of your online business, whether it's retail arbitrage, online arbitrage, wholesale sourcing, trade show sourcing or private label development and sales. In fact, adopting some good outsourcing principles can be helpful in whatever business that you're in, whether it's online or offline.

Our History in Book-selling

My family and I have been selling new and lightly used books online for over 10 years. When I was in college over 10 years ago, I would sell my old textbooks on a site called half.com, remember that site? Before Amazon was Amazon. If I ever needed a book, Half.com is where I went to find it. For those of you who don't know Half.com was/is a company owned by Ebay.com. It's still in operation (now half.ebay.com) but obviously doesn't sell the volume of books that Amazon does every day.

In 2010, we started selling books, part-time, on Amazon. We would grab a few books at the local Goodwill, usually the $.15 clearance books and then cross our fingers that at least a couple of them would be profitable when we looked them up on the computer at home. As you can guess, we hardly made any money since the really popular used books (which we assumed would be worth money) tend to over-saturate the market and the horrible hard to find books, well no-one cared about those when they were printed and sadly no-one cares about those books now. So, we needed to figure out a more efficient way to figure out whether or not a book was worth purchasing for resale, which leads us to Step #1 of Book Flipping for Passive Income (which I'll get to in a moment).

Books: The Gateway Drug

Books are a great place to start. If you were to run an informal poll on one of the various Facebook forums, you would find that an overwhelming number of successful online sellers cut their teeth selling books. Finding books is easy, the profit margins are exceptional, and this will give you and your online business the necessary momentum to successfully launch into other categories down the road. Once you've tasted success in books, you can move into other categories such as: Toys & Games, Grocery, Health & Beauty, DVD, Sporting Goods, Baby, etc. You'll be able to take the lessons learned from book sourcing and apply them to any item that has a barcode.

If you follow my plan and, not only start and grow your online book selling business, but fully outsource it as well, you'll have the money and the freedom to expand into other areas of online selling.

Here is what many sellers consider the natural progression of sourcing locations:
1.   Low or No Cost Sources
2.   Offline Retail
3.   Online Retail
4.   Liquidation
5.   National Wholesale
6.   International Wholesale
7.   Private Label

So, you start off with Low or No Cost Sources of inventory and then you progress your way down the line. There are a couple of things to consider; you could just stop at books. There would be nothing wrong with that; in fact, it may be the best option for you and your family. As I have previously discussed, there's great money to be made selling books alone. But, if you did decide to expand, I've provided you with some options. Also, feel free to shake up the order of this list to suit your own strengths and experiences.

Okay, back to books (for now).

Step #1: Acquire a Barcode Scanning Device

"The number one benefit of information technology is that it empowers people to do what they want to do. It lets people be creative. It lets people be productive. It lets people learn things they didn't think they could learn before, and so in a sense it is all about potential."
-Steve Ballmer former CEO of Microsoft

Important Tools of Technology

So what books sell well on Amazon? Well, that's a great question! I could spend chapters telling you ins and outs of the used book-selling industry, but that's not the point of this book. We read the book *Barcode Booty: How I Found and Sold $2 Million of 'Junk' on eBay and Amazon, and You Can Too, Using Your Phone,* by Steve Weber and our brains exploded. As I'm writing this, I see that this book is on Kindle Unlimited and that it can be purchased on Kindle for $2.99! We never thought of utilizing technology to make our book-selling gig more profitable and more efficient! We downloaded some free scanning apps and went to work. Having the power of live-streaming info at our finger-tips paid off in a huge way!

No longer did we have to guess whether or not a book was worth re-selling, our phone would tell us! Who knew that the book *Beading with Brick Stitch* by Fitzgerald was worth money!? Well, we didn't then but we do now thanks to technology (Sold yesterday for $12.95).

Scanning barcodes with our smart phone was great, it was obviously a huge improvement on what we were accustomed to, but it did have its draw-backs. 1) The smart phone apps only work when you have reception, and 2) often times we have to wait way to long while the app loaded the AZ listing (when we did have reception). We knew that to make the book-selling business work, we need to scan in volumes. If only 1 out of every 10 books met our criteria, the faster we scan 10 books, the faster we find the one.

To make a long story short, I was dinking around on YouTube doing some good ole' fashion research, and I stumbled across "PDA Scanning Programs". I think it was Rob Anderson from Dollar Moves (on YouTube) that enlightened me. For those of you who weren't born in the 80's, a PDA (Personal Digital Assistant) was a device that was popular in the 90s that mainly functioned as a personal organizer that also provided email and limited internet access.

PDA Scanning

We discovered that there were data companies out there (NeatOscan and ASellerTool) that would sell data subscriptions that people could download onto their PDA devices so that they could have access to the entire Book category (prices and rank on Amazon), with lightning fast precision, whether there was cell reception or not! And when I say lightning fast I mean it, I could scan 10 books on the PDA faster than I could scan one on the smart phone. Now, I know that cell service and Smartphone apps are a lot faster now than they were a few years ago, but PDA scanning equipment is still much faster.

We bought a used PDA (off Craigslist for $40), a ScanFob Bluetooth scanner ($350) and paid $40 for our first month subscription to ASellerTool.

Nowadays, when purchasing an additional PDA unit, we bought a lightly used Dell Axim x51v package from ASellerTool Inc on eBay.com (here's a link to their store http://www.ebay.com/usr/asellertoolinc?_trksid=p2047675.l2559). These range in price from $115 to $300 and they come preloaded with the Amazon media database as well as all of the necessary ASellerTool software. Also included is a 2GB memory card and a socket barcode laser scanner that fits perfectly at the top of the unit. Before I move on, I want to spend some time touching on the various products and applications that both ASellerTool and NeatOScan have to offer.

ASellerTool gives this information to you in the palm of your hand

Speed is the key to being successful in this business, and AsellerTool's programs offer just that. Here is the information that you'll rapidly use to make a quick buying decision:

Book Title – at the top of the PDA readout will be a shortened title, which will help to ensure that you are looking at the correct book.

Price, Condition, and Quantity – In a series of color coded horizontal columns, you'll find the price, condition, and quantity information regarding your online competition. More on how to read this PDA layout is included in a different chapter. Price will automatically include postage so you can gain a better understanding of what your MF competition is selling their books for.

Sales Rank – At the bottom left of the PDA layout, you'll see the Amazon sales rank. In a future chapter, I'll walk you through determining whether or not a sales rank is a good sales rank.

Number of Offers – The total number of used and new offers will be conveniently displayed at the bottom of the screen. This is helpful when considering whether or not to purchase a book that's on the edge of the criteria. If there's an overwhelming amount of competition, maybe you should skip it. On the other hand, if the competition is scarce, maybe the book is worth taking a chance.

ASellerTool has three different programs. They offer Android/iPhone Scouting, PDA Scouting and Amazon Batch Listing.

The **Android/iPhone Scouting** program is very similar to the downloadable Amazon database for the PDA but it's formatted for a smart phone. You are able to download all of the necessary info right onto your phone without the extra equipment. FBAScan is the name of the app that you can download onto your device and it will do live or local searches depending on whether or not you have service. You can use your Smartphone's camera to scan barcodes, or you could purchase a Blue tooth Laser scanner and sync it up with your device for quick scanning.

The only downfall to this option is that you are downloading a rather large program onto your smart phone. Do you really want to tie-up, up to 2GB of memory on your phone? But, on the flip-side, there are some benefits to being able to have access to live and/or local Amazon data all on one device. I must admit, it would be rather convenient. You may want to look into purchasing this program for your book-scouts and just have them download the program right onto their phone. This way you wouldn't have to worry about lost or broken equipment (although this hasn't been a problem for us at all).

They also offer a **PDA Scouting Program**. Here, you have a couple of options. You can use your own PDA or you can rent one from ASellerTool, which is an intriguing option. On their website you can:

1. **Buy a used PDA** for $499 (with the 5E2 scanner) or $599 (with the 5P scanner), and these packages both come with four months of service ($120 value).
2. **Lease the Dell X51 PDA for FREE** ($70 refundable deposit), and **buy the laser scanner**. This package will cost you either $299 (5E2) or $399 (5P). This includes one month of free service.
3. Sign up for the **"Full Rental Package"** which is $14.95/month for the hardware and $30/month for the software subscription ($45/total for one device)

When we originally signed up for ASellerTool a few years back they only had one option, which was that you needed to own your own PDA and scanner and then you would pay them for access to the Amazon database. We currently own 4 active PDAs that are used among all of our Book-Shopping people which brings the monthly rate per unit down a bit, but if you're just getting started out and you decide to go the PDA route, you may want to explore these other options.

Included with both of their scouting programs is their down-loadable Amazon Batch Listing software (I'll talk about batch listing in Step #6)

ProfitSourcing.com
Subscription Pricing

2. Standard   Subscribe

(Local Database + Limited Live Searches + Amazon Batch Listing Software)

Number of Devices	Every Month	Every 6 Month 5% off	Every 12 Month 15% off
1	$30	$171	$306
2	$50	$285	$510
3	$70	$399	$714
4	$85	$484.50	$867

Figure 8

For one device, whether it's a smart-phone or PDA, they charge
$30/month on a month to month plan (Figure 8). You can also commit to
multiple months in order to save a little more. As you grow your book-
selling business and add multiple devices to your subscription,
ASellerTool will give you a nice break on price.

Live Scouting

ASellerTool also offers **Live Scouting** on its app **FBAScan**. If you are interested in doing some retail arbitrage and would like to do an in-store, live evaluation, you could us the FBAScan app. Of the four main phone scouting apps, I think that this one comes in last. I would rank them as follows: 1) Scoutify, 2) ScanPower, 3) Profit Bandit, and 4) FBAScan. Their live scanning app just doesn't have the features that the other ones offer. But it's always nice to have a back-up app on your device, so with these scanning packages, you'll also get limited access to FBAScan live on your phone.

Again, for more information go to www.asellertool.com.
For a short video on how AST works, check out this Youtube video: https://www.youtube.com/watch?v=xOUH3VkTiGc– or simply search ASellerTool on Youtube to find a plethora of video reviews.

neatOscan

NeatOscan, a Minnesota based company, also offers some programs very similar with what ASellerTool has to offer. They do not have a PDA and/or barcode scanner leasing program, but you can purchase new equipment (although it seems rather expensive). Their subscription programs offer options for both PDA and smart-phone downloads

Standard Service Level
All standard accounts come with our unlimited data updates and free tech support during business hours.

# of Licenses	Monthly	Quarterly
1 license	$50.00 per license	$142.50 per license
2 licenses	$47.50 per license	$135.00 per license
3 licenses	$45.00 per license	$127.50 per license
4 licenses	$42.50 per license	$120.00 per license
5+ license	$40.00 per license	$112.50 per license

Figure 9

The monthly subscription fees are significantly higher than what ASellerTool has to offer (Figure 9), but notice that you do get a slight discount for paying for quarterly and not monthly. To be honest, I've never used NeatOscan before and wasn't able to dig up any solid info on their website in regards to any advantage that they may have over the competition.

NeatOscan also offers some Inventory Management and Evaluator programs that could help your Amazon business in other ways, and could be worth looking into. They claim that they provide a "turn-key" listing and inventory management set up, but in order to get pricing you'll need to chat with a customer service representative.

For more information on the services that NeatOscan offers go to www.neatoscan.com
For a short video on how NeatOscan works check out this Youtube: https://www.youtube.com/watch?v=mUfvdwqZWaQ or keyword search "NeatOscan" on Youtube for more options.

Conclusion

After getting set up with our PDA scanner we sold books for some nice part-time income for a couple of years. We even traveled to some of the bigger national book-selling events, and were able to make some nice scores.

Shortly after we began selling on Amazon we realized that we liked nearly everything about the business except the fulfillment. With a wife and six kids at home to care for the last thing that we had time for was packing and shipping out books every day. Also, we were looking forward to scaling up our online business so that we could have the freedom of owning our own business, without being in bondage to it. The freedom to take long vacations and to get up and travel at a moment notice. There's no way this was going to happen if we were required to be home every other day to handle all of the logistics of our business. This leads us to Step #2 in...

Recap:
Step#1 Acquire a Barcode Scanning Device

Step #2: Outsource With FBA

"Just set it and forget it!"
Ron Popeil, founder of RONCO,
a billion dollar rotisserie chicken roaster company

Not only can you call on Amazon to assist you with order fulfillment, they also will handle all of your storage needs. Although we planned on sourcing books that would sell fast, we understood that many of the books that we were buying may have to sit on the shelf for a while (more on the value of "Long Tail" books to come). We have books in our inventory that have been there for years, waiting for the right Amazon shopper to come around. We started running out of storage room at home. Plus, book selling is a numbers game. The more quality books you have in your inventory the more books you'll sell per week. It's pretty simple. Anyway, we needed to find a solution to both of these problems: 1) we didn't want to be a slave to our home, spending valuable time every day fulfilling customer orders and, 2) we needed a practical place to store our books before they sold (our little ranch style house wasn't cutting it). That's when we heard about F.B.A.

FBA is the Solution

You may be saying F.B.What? F.B.A. Is an acronym for "Fulfillment by Amazon". With FBA You store your products in Amazon's fulfillment centers, and they pick, pack, ship and provide customer service for these products. Happily this solution solved both of our problems.

What is Amazon FBA, and why should I care?

That's a great question. I'm glad you asked! FBA has revolutionized the way that little home-based sellers can sell on Amazon, as well as, other online marketplaces. Here's how it works. You, the seller, find a handful of items that you decide you would like to sell online. You go through the traditional steps of listing the items on Amazon, but instead of choosing to Merchant Fulfill the item, which is the traditional way of selling things, you instead select the FBA option.

Typically, you would list and item for sale on Amazon, and as soon as you submitted the listing, the said item would be immediately available for sale. Buyers on Amazon would have the option of purchasing your item from among all the sellers on that specific product page. If you are the "chosen one", and a customer purchases your item then you would get a message from Amazon, prompting you to ship your item to the customer. You, the seller/fulfiller, handle all customer service, pack and ship the item to the customer, and handle all customer returns, as well as, any other fulfillment related issues.

Here's where FBA is different

When Amazon fulfills your items, your items are not available for sale upon listing them. Instead, you are prompted to print special barcodes to adhere to your individual items in order to differentiate your products from the products of other sellers at the fulfillment center. Next, you're instructed to pack all of your items, in bulk, into boxes and ship them to an Amazon fulfillment center near you (well, I hope you get one close; sometimes, they may ask you to have your stuff shipped across country). As you work through the process, you are offered "Amazon Partnered Shipping Rates", which means that you can take advantage of the super low rates that Amazon has with UPS (Ground tends to cost between 30 – 40 cents per pound for us, which is incredibly cheap).

Once this large box of listed goods arrives at its destination, Amazon will shelf your items in one of its massive, state-of-the-art warehouses. Once this happens, your items will then become available for sale. So, when a customer buys your item, Amazon will go and retrieve your specific, specially labeled item and ship it to the customer.

Here are the benefits of FBA:

Amazon handles all of the logistics, customer service & returns, which will, in turn, free up a ton of your time. They will be able to offer your customers two-day and overnight shipping on all of your orders. Also, all of your items are now eligible for Super-Saver Shipping benefits, which mean that if a customer spends over $35, they receive free two-day shipping or a much discounted overnight shipping option. Amazon Prime members will be able to purchase your items and have them shipped in two-days, guaranteed, for free! This is an absolute game-changer! World-class logistics will set you apart from your MF (Merchant Fulfilled) competition in a huge way!

Now, when you find yourself in competition with another Amazon seller, but you're FBA and they're MF, you'll have the advantage. Amazon customers, such as me, have become accustomed to Amazon's super fast shipping and world-class customer service, and this encourages me to buy a Prime Eligible item over a Merchant Fulfilled item whenever I get the chance, even if the Prime Eligible item is priced much higher.

Oftentimes, Amazon shoppers, when looking to make a purchase, will sort all of the offers by selecting the Prime Eligible items-only button near the top of the page. This option single-handedly eliminates all of the MF competition with one click. Although Amazon has not disclosed the number of Prime Members they have currently collected, they have hinted that as many as 60% of their online customers have signed up for Prime Membership.

Besides the main benefit, being able to utilize Amazon's logistics and customer service, there are many others worth considering:

- FBA sellers have a greater probability of winning the Buy Box, even if they're not the lowest price.
- FBA sellers open their market to the growing trend of Amazon Prime-only shoppers.
- FBA allows you to spend less time packing and shipping and more time focusing on what you love.

The last benefit that I mentioned is key. Yesterday, according to our Seller Central page, we sold and shipped over 50 items, all FBA. These items were sold and shipped while I was doing a variety of important things: sleeping, spending time with my family, enjoying a beautiful day, building my Amazon business in different ways, and writing this post.

If I would have had to ship each of these items myself, it would have carved out a decent chunk of my day. Think of it this way; If each item needed a box, invoice, and shipping label, and the estimated time that it would take me to get this done amounted to about 5 minutes per item, it would have taken me over 4 hours just to fulfill the day's orders (5 minutes x 50 items)! If we ship an average of 500 items per week, we're talking about over 41 hours of time spent boxing and shipping. Do you see that by outsourcing your logistics to Amazon, you are able to free a ton of time?

Now, some of you more experienced sellers may say that it shouldn't take 5 minutes per box, but even if we developed a system that cut that estimate in half, we would still be devoting way too much time, in my estimation, to packing and shipping. Why not let Amazon do it for you?

The burden of packing and shipping individual boxes limits the scalability of your business; by outsourcing this task to Amazon, the experts, it frees valuable time that can be invested in others areas.

Fees for FBA

The next question that people typically ask at this time in the conversation is, "Well, FBA sounds wonderful, but how much do you need to pay them for this service?" That's another good question.
Amazon's fee structure is differentiated across selling categories; if you are interested in comparing the fees for MF vs. FBA, check out Amazon's FBA Revenue Calculator.

Just for perspective, over the last 6 months we paid $5.35/book in Amazon fees. Our average book sold for $14.41, so Amazon takes a little more than 1/3rd of the sale price for books priced around this price-point. Remember that this $5.35 also includes shipping to the customer.

But, don't let the fees scare you. Think of it this way. For most businesses, the #1 expense that they pay every year is for marketing. Marketing is what brings in customers and creates opportunities to make sales. When you sell things on Amazon, they will handle all of the marketing. So, when I noticed that Amazon took a 30% commission on an item that I sold the other day, I wasn't upset. I figure that a 30% commission for all my marketing and logistical services is not too shabby.

Amazon is the largest, most visited, online marketplace in the world, and they have invited you and me to come and sell our goods for no upfront cost. It would be like the busiest mall in America offering you a storefront rent free, and instead, only asking for a reasonable commission. Oh yeah, and they would provide all of the advertising to keep new customers flowing through the doors. Also, Amazon doesn't charge selling fees until after the item has sold.

Selling a Low priced book (MF vs. FBA)

Everyone wants to know how much Amazon is going to take from them when they sell a book, and this is a fair question. The short answer is they will typically take between 30-40% of the sale price. The lower the price of the item, the higher the percentage of the sale is allocated to Amazon fees. So, if your ASP (Average Sale Price) is high, the percentage in fees that Amazon takes will be lower than if you are selling books cheap. Let's take a look at Amazon's fee breakdown. When you sell a book, fees vary per book based on size and price. Let's pretend that we'd like to sell the book, *The Artist's Way* by Julia Cameron (Figure 10).

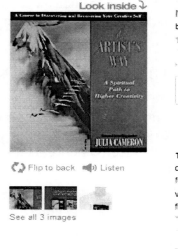

Figure 10

As you may have noticed from this listing, there are a lot of other sellers selling this book: 297 Used offers + 107 New offers + 2 Collectable Offers = 406 Total Offers. If you were to scroll down the page a bit, you'd see that this book has an Amazon Best Sellers Rank of 606 in Books (Figure 11). This is truly a remarkably ranked book. Normally, I'd be worried about trying to compete with so many other online sellers, but since the rank is so good, as long as I can offer my book at a competitive price, I'd be happy to sell on this listing.

Product Details

Paperback: 237 pages
Publisher: Jeremy P. Tarcher/Putnam; 10 Anv edition (March 4, 2002)
Language: English
ISBN-10: 1585421464
ISBN-13: 978-1585421466
Product Dimensions: 7.5 x 0.7 x 9 inches
Shipping Weight: 1.2 pounds (View shipping rates and policies)
Average Customer Review: ★★★★☆ (820 customer reviews)
● **Amazon Best Sellers Rank:** #606 in Books (See Top 100 in Books) ●
　　　　#3 in Books > Arts & Photography > **Individual Artists**
　　　　#3 in Books > Religion & Spirituality > Worship & Devotion > **Inspirational**
　　　　#5 in Books > Health, Fitness & Dieting > Psychology & Counseling > **Creativity & Genius**

Figure 11

You may also have noticed that the book doesn't seem to be very high priced. In fact, this particular book is being sold in New condition by Amazon for $9.27 + tax (Figure 12):

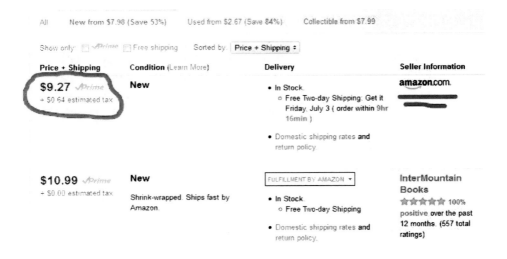

Figure 12

But, don't let that discourage you. Let's assume that our copy is in Used Very Good Condition (more on Amazon's Condition Guidelines in a bit). Here's a look at the top four used offers for this book and their respective conditions (Figure 13):

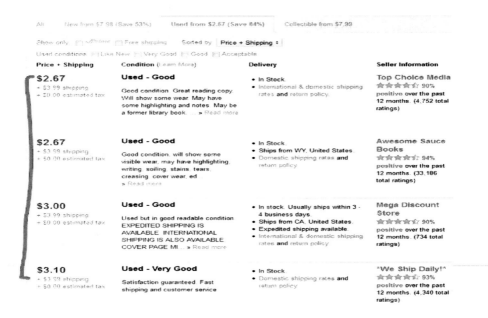

The top four Used offers for this book are MF or Merchant Fulfilled. This means that they are not being housed and shipped from an Amazon fulfillment center, but that they are coming to you directly from the 3rd party merchant. This can be discerned by the $3.99 shipping charge that will be paid in addition to the book price.

If I was going to sell my Used Very Good book Merchant fulfilled, I would match the other Very Good copy at $3.10 (+$3.99 shipping).

Before we determine a competitive FBA price for this book, let's figure out the fees that you would pay if you sold this book and fulfilled it yourself. The best place to get an accurate layout of Amazon fees by listing is using the FBA Revenue Calculator.

After entering the book's information, here's the screen that comes up. Next, I will enter in all of my expenses (Figure 14).

Figure 14

In the **Item Price** box, I'll put in **$3.10**, since this is the price I plan on selling this book for.

In the **Shipping** box, I'll put **$3.99**. Even though Amazon will be collecting and giving me $3.99, I think that I should be able to ship this book either media mail or first class for just under $2. This means that I can pocket the extra $1.99 (hey, every little bit helps).

In the **Outbound Shipping** box, I'll put **$2.00,** which is what I estimate shipping to cost,

In the **Inbound Shipping** box, I'll enter **$2.00,** which will represent the cost of this book to me. Let's say that we found this book at thrift-store for $2.00.

I hit the **Calculate** button, and here's what our profits would look like (Figure 15):

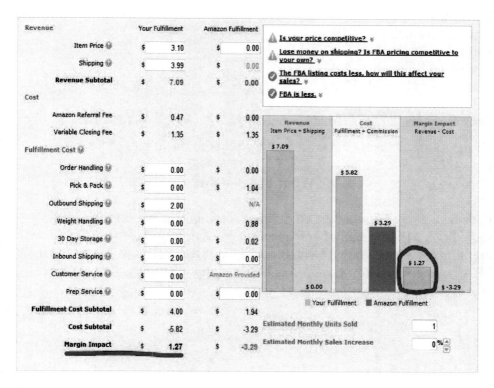

Figure 15

At this price, we could expect to make a net profit of $1.27 if we Merchant Fulfilled this item. I don't know about you, but $1.27 doesn't seem worth it to me. I mean, we not only have to find the book, but it is on us to clean it, box it, and ship it to the customer. Typically, it's wise to look for books that can make a greater profit. Also, for simplicity, we are not adding additional expenses that are common when running a merchant fulfilled business such as packing tape, necessary equipment, subscription services, boxes, ink, and paper.

Financial Breakdown:

Revenue
Sale Price: $3.10
Shipping Credit: $3.99

Expenses
Amazon Referral Fee: $0.47
Variable Closing Fee: $1.35
Outbound Shipping: $2.00
Cost of Goods Sold: $2.00

Total Revenue $7.09 – Total Expenses $5.82 = **$1.27 Net Profit.**

Of the total sale, Amazon would take about 25.7% in fees ($1.82)

What about FBA?

Let's take a look at what we could expect to make if we sold this very same book FBA instead of MF. Because we can sell FBA books at premium over MF books, I want to sort the Used offers, so I only see my FBA competition. You can do this by checking the "Show Only Prime" box at the top of the offer page (Figure 16).

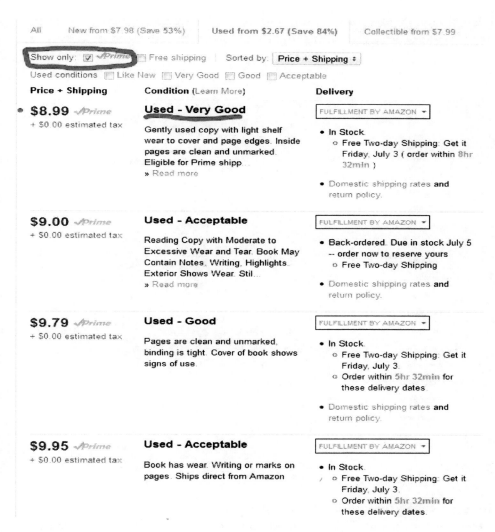

Figure 16

If I were pricing this book to sell via FBA, I would match the low Very Good price at $8.99 with free shipping. Actually, I just sold a copy of this book last month for $9.95, so when pricing your books, you may want to start high and then bring the price down over time. Since Amazon currently is selling this book for $9.27, they must have been out of stock when my copy was purchased, which does happen from time to time.

Let's plug our same information into the FBA Revenue Calculator using our new sales price and some slightly altered expenses (Figure 17):

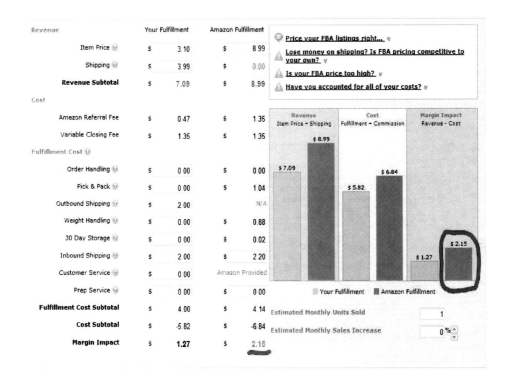

Figure 17

Item Price: $8.99 (our FBA sale price)

Inbound Shipping: $2.20 (to send your books into Amazon costs about $.20/book. I've also included the $2.00 cost of the book in this box as well).

Let's crunch some numbers!

Financial Breakdown:

Revenue
Sale Price: $8.99

Shipping Credit: $0.00

Expenses
Amazon Referral Fee: $1.35
Variable Closing Fee: $1.35
Pick & Pack: $1.04
Weight Handling: $0.88
30 Day Storage: $0.02
Inbound Shipping: $2.20

Total Cost of Goods Sold: $6.84

Total Revenue $8.99 – Total Expenses $6.84 = **$2.15 Net Profit.**

Of the total sale, Amazon take would about 51% in fees ($4.64).

51%!! Keep in mind that $4.64 includes the cost to ship the book to the end user and spend the man-hours to ensure that the customer is happy. The number that is most interesting is the Total Net Profit between the two fulfillment options:

$1.27 Net Profit when Fulfilled by Merchant
$2.15 Net Profit when Fulfilled by Amazon

Even though the fees nearly doubled as a percentage of the sale, 25% to 51%, the Net Profit is better if you sell this book via FBA.

More Examples

I hope that you don't feel like I'm beating a dead horse on this issue, but I'd like to crunch the numbers once again; this time with a more expensive listings. Amazon fees become much more reasonable when you get over $15. Here are some more examples:

Ottoman Women Paperback – December 20, 2007

by Asli Sancar ▾ (Author)

★★★★★ ▾ 4 customer reviews

ISBN-13: 978-1597841153 | ISBN-10: 1597841153

Buy New

Price: $26.96 ✓Prime

33 New from $17.99 | 33 Used from $1.86

	Amazon Price	New from	Used from
▸ Paperback	$26.96 ✓Prime	$17.99	$1.86

Figure 18

This book, *Ottoman Women* by Asli Sancar, is selling for **$26.96** in **New condition**. Let's say that we have a copy that's in **Used-Good** condition. If we decided to Merchant Fulfill this book, we would price it at **$1.88** to match our MF competition (Figure 19):

$1.88

+ $3.99 shipping
+ $0.00 estimated tax

Used - Good

OVERALL USED CONDITION, ALL PAGES AND COVER ARE INTACT, SPINE MAY SHOW SINGS OF WEAR. PAGES MAY INCLUDE LIMITED NOTES AND HIG...

» Read more

Figure 19

If we were to sell this book in Used-Good via FBA, we would price our copy a bit higher at **$12.88**. This **Used-Good** price just so happens to be the lowest Prime option on the listing (Figure 20).

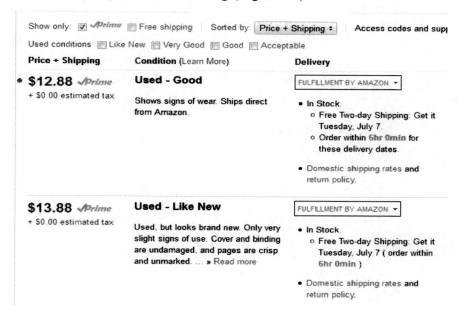

Figure 20

You may be wondering, "Would someone in their right mind buy a book for $12.88 FBA when they could buy the same book, in the same condition MF for $5.87 (1.88+3.99)?" The answer is yes! The typical Amazon book shopper does it all of the time.

Let's breakdown the fees:

Revenue	Your Fulfillment	Amazon Fulfillment
Item Price	$ 1.88	$ 12.88
Shipping	$ 3.99	$ 0.00
Revenue Subtotal	$ 5.87	$ 12.88
Cost		
Amazon Referral Fee	$ 0.28	$ 1.93
Variable Closing Fee	$ 1.35	$ 1.35
Fulfillment Cost		
Order Handling	$ 0.00	$ 0.00
Pick & Pack	$ 0.00	$ 1.04
Outbound Shipping	$ 2.00	N/A
Weight Handling	$ 0.00	$ 0.88
30 Day Storage	$ 0.00	$ 0.01
Inbound Shipping	$ 2.00	$ 2.20
Customer Service	$ 0.00	Amazon Provided
Prep Service	$ 0.00	$ 0.00
Fulfillment Cost Subtotal	$ 4.00	$ 4.13
Cost Subtotal	$ -5.63	$ -7.41
Margin Impact	$ **0.24**	$ 5.47

Figure 21

Here, I entered the same expenses from the last example (Figure 21), which takes into consideration the cost to acquire the book ($2.00) and the cost to ship the book ($2.00 for MF and $0.20 for FBA).

$1.63 Amazon Fees when Fulfilled by Merchant at $1.88 (does not include shipping credit)
$5.21 Amazon Fees when Fulfilled by Amazon at $12.88

$0.24 Net Profit when Fulfilled by Merchant
$5.47 Net Profit when Fulfilled by Amazon

So you see, some books that are hardly profitable to a 3rd party seller, who Merchant Fulfills them, may have profitability for the FBA seller, and since most Amazon book sellers still Merchant Fulfill their books, here's an opportunity to give your business a competitive advantage.

Next Example:

A Teacher's Guide to the Multigenre Research Project: Everything You Need to Get Started Paperback – February 21, 2006
by Melinda Putz ▾ (Author)
⭐⭐⭐⭐⭐ ▾ 8 customer reviews
ISBN-13: 978-0325007854   ISBN-10: 0325007853

Buy New   **Rent**
Price: $30.38 ✓Prime   Price: $16.56 ✓Prime

8 New from $30.38   20 Used from $20.06

Rent from	Amazon Price	New from	Used from

Figure 22

Let's say that we would like to sell this book in Used-Good condition (Figure 22). According to the listing, the MF and the FBA price are essentially identical (Figure 23).

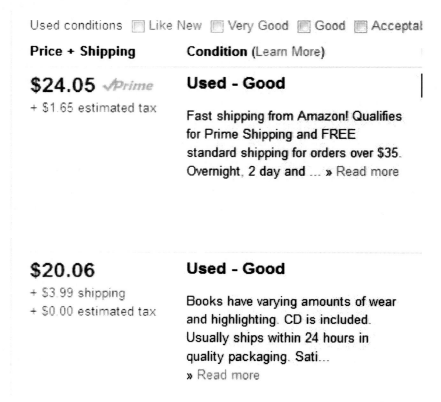

Figure 23

Note – Depending upon where the buyer is located and from where the book is being shipped will determine any sales tax.

If we were thinking about selling this book in Used-Good condition, for simplicity's sake, let's set our sale price at $24.05 for both MF and FBA.

ProfitSourcing.com

Revenue	Your Fulfillment	Amazon Fulfillment
Item Price	$ 20.06	$ 24.05
Shipping	$ 3.99	$ 0.00
Revenue Subtotal	$ 24.05	$ 24.05
Cost		
Amazon Referral Fee	$ 3.01	$ 3.61
Variable Closing Fee	$ 1.35	$ 1.35
Fulfillment Cost		
Order Handling	$ 0.00	$ 0.00
Pick & Pack	$ 0.00	$ 1.04
Outbound Shipping	$ 2.00	N/A
Weight Handling	$ 0.00	$ 0.50
30 Day Storage	$ 0.00	$ 0.01
Inbound Shipping	$ 2.00	$ 2.20
Customer Service	$ 0.00	Amazon Provided
Prep Service	$ 0.00	$ 0.00
Fulfillment Cost Subtotal	$ 4.00	$ 3.75
Cost Subtotal	$ -8.36	$ -8.71
Margin Impact	$ **15.69**	$ 15.34

Figure 24

Here, I entered the same expenses from the last examples (Figure 24), which takes into consideration the cost to acquire the book ($2.00) and the cost to ship the book ($2.00 for MF and $0.20 for FBA).

$4.36 Amazon Fees when Fulfilled by Merchant at $24.05 ($20.06+$3.99). (Does not include shipping credit)
$6.51 Amazon Fees when Fulfilled by Amazon at $24.05

$15.69 Net Profit when Fulfilled by Merchant
$15.34 Net Profit when Fulfilled by Amazon

If you MF'd this book, you'd make a whopping **$0.35 more,** according to my calculations. The alternative would be to sell your book FBA and put your book in the exclusive Prime Eligible category, which I'm confident will open up your customer base in a big way. Outsourcing the logistics will not only help you increase sales, but it will free your time to do more sourcing or work on other areas of your business.

Let's quickly look at a few more examples before we move on:

 **Mastering Your Inner Game**
ASIN: 073600176X
Product Dimensions: 9.02 X 6.02 X 0.69 inches
Shipping Weight: 0.44 pounds

See Product Details 🗗

Figure 25

Let's say that we have this book, *Mastering Your Inner Game* (Figure 25), in Used-Very Good condition. The comparable prices would be $8.95 (+ $3.99 shipping) MF and $70.84 FBA (no joke!).

$2.68 Amazon Fees when Fulfilled by Merchant at $8.95 (about 30% in fees)
$13.53 Amazon Fees when Fulfilled by Amazon at $70.84 (about 20% in fees)

$6.25 Net Profit when Fulfilled by Merchant
$55.11 Net Profit when Fulfilled by Amazon

A Place of Interest
ASIN: 1414122810
Product Dimensions: 8.6 X 5.5 X 0.4 inches
Shipping Weight: 0.3 pounds

See Product Details ↻

Figure 26

If we wanted to sell this book, *A Place of Interest* (Figure 26), in Used-
Very Good condition, the comparable prices would be $12.00 (+$3.99
shipping) MF and $68.19 FBA. This is another big jump in price to be
sure. But it looks like the $12.00 MF price is sort of an outlier; all of the
other used prices for this book are hovering around the upper $60s.

$3.15 Amazon Fees when Fulfilled by Merchant at $12.00 (about 26% in
fees)
$13.13 Amazon Fees when Fulfilled by Amazon at $68.19 (about 19% in
fees)

$8.84 Net Profit when Fulfilled by Merchant
$52.86 Net Profit when Fulfilled by Amazon

Crush It!: Why NOW Is the Time to Cash In on Your Passion
ASIN: 0061914177
Product Dimensions: 8.35 X 5.59 X 0.79 inches
Shipping Weight: 0.57 pounds

See Product Details ↻

Figure 27

If we wanted to sell this book, *Crush It!* by Gary Vaynerchuk (Figure 27), in Used-Good condition, the comparable sale prices would be $3.00 (+$3.99 shipping) MF and $9.99 FBA. This is a more typical price spread between a book that is sold MF and a book that is sold FBA.

$1.80 Amazon Fees when Fulfilled by Merchant at $3.00 (about 60% in fees)
$4.53 Amazon Fees when Fulfilled by Amazon at $9.99 (about 45% in fees)

$1.19 Net Profit when Fulfilled by Merchant
$3.26 Net Profit when Fulfilled by Amazon

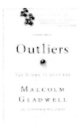

Outliers: The Story of Success
ASIN: 0316017930
Product Dimensions: 8.3 X 5.5 X 1 inches
Shipping Weight: 0.65 pounds

See Product Details ⏷

Figure 28

If we wanted to sell this book, *Outliers* by Malcolm Gladwell (Figure 28), in Used Very Good condition, we find that the FBA price is actually lower than the MF price + shipping. The comparables on this listing would have us price our copy for $7.63 (+ $3.99 shipping) MF and $9.98 FBA. I don't think that any customer in their right mind would pass over a cheaper FBA offer to go to the 2nd page and buy from an MF seller at a slightly higher price, but here are the numbers.

$2.49 Amazon Fees when Fulfilled by Merchant at $7.63 (about 33% in fees)
$4.53 Amazon Fees when Fulfilled by Amazon at $9.98 (about 45% in fees)

$5.13 Net Profit when Fulfilled by Merchant
$3.25 Net Profit when Fulfilled by Amazon

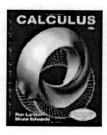

Calculus
ASIN: 1285057090
Product Dimensions: 11.1 X 8.8 X 1.9 inches
Shipping Weight: 6.5 pounds

See Product Details ⌐

Figure 29

Let's take a look at a higher priced textbook to see how the numbers pan out. If we had a copy of this book, *Calculus* by Larson & Edwards (Figure 29), in Used Very Good Condition, we would list it for $149.95 (+ $3.99 shipping) MF and $163.98 FBA.

$23.84 Amazon Fees when Fulfilled by Merchant at $149.95 (about 16% in fees)
$29.97 Amazon Fees when Fulfilled by Amazon at $163.98 (about 18% in fees)

$126.10 Net Profit when Fulfilled by Merchant
$131.81 Net Profit when Fulfilled by Amazon

As you can see, the higher the price of the item that you are selling, the less percentage that Amazon takes. Hopefully these examples have given you a clearer understanding of Amazon's fee structures for both MF and FBA books. The important thing is, as an FBA seller, you can typically make up for the additional fees by charging more, which in my mind, makes the switch from MF to FBA a no-brainer!

In Conclusion

Essentially this is how it works. You buy a bunch of books at a thrift-store that you are determined to sell on Amazon for a profit. Next you clean and prep these books for sale by scraping of any labels and price-tags that don't belong and doing other things to quickly make the books look nice for your prospective customers. After the prepping is finished, you will now need to list these particular books on Amazon. By scanning the book's bar-code (usually on the back of the book) or entering the UPC/ISBN by

hand you will be able to pull up the Amazon listing page for that book and then let Amazon know that you have one of those books in which you'd like to sell, and which condition it's in (more on the particulars of book listing in Step #6). You'll print unique barcodes for each of your books on address sized labels and then you will box all of your books, in bulk, and ship them off to a designated Amazon fulfillment center (benefiting from Amazon's partnered shipping rates with UPS, which costs us about $.34/pound for Ground).

Once Amazon receives this box of books they will shelf them in their state of the art warehouse and make them available for sale, for the first time, on Amazon.com. Now, when a customer orders your particular book, Amazon employees, or robots, will retrieve your exact copy and have it shipped to your customer. Since all of the books that you will have for sale will be at an Amazon warehouse, Amazon will guarantee that Prime or Super-Saver shipping eligible customers will have the book in 2 days or less.

Understanding Amazon Sales Rank

Sales rank is one criterion that generally gets people bent out of shape. Some sellers over-emphasize sales rank out of confusion of what sale rank actually means, and others just follow the pack. There are over 2 million other 3rd party sellers selling their wares on Amazon; it makes it easier to out-sell and out-hustle your competition if you fully understand the game that you're playing. So, let's spend some time talking rank, so you can have an edge over the other online sellers.

If you spend any time in the online seller forums, you'll find that one of the most common questions is "What's a good rank?" On eBay, we have the ability to search for completed listings, but since we don't have that concrete past sales information on Amazon, many have turned to Amazon's Sales Rank as an equal alternative (but don't be deceived, it's not the same!).

Here is a very helpful sales rank chart that SellerEngine.com shared in one of their blog posts (Figure 30):

Category	Number of Items	Top 10%
Beauty	1,910,654	191,000 and lower
Books	36,221,882	3,622,000 and lower
Cell Phones & Accessories	10,085,052	1,000,000 and lower
Clothing & Accessories	4,414,895	441,000 and lower
Electronics	22,638,305	2,263,000 and lower
Grocery & Gourmet Food	634,313	63,400 and lower
Health & Personal Care	4,346,934	434,000 and lower
Home & Kitchen	15,335,938	1,533,000 and lower
Office Products	3,659,501	365,000 and lower
Sports & Outdoors	17,190,720	1,719,000 and lower
Toys & Games	2,560,438	256,000 and lower

Figure 30

This chart, which was last updated in May of 2014, gives you an idea of how many items Amazon has for sale. But, let's take a look at the Book category. There are 36+ million active book listings on Amazon.

An active listing is simply a listing for a particular book that has sold at least one copy. If an item hasn't sold a single unit, its rank will be zero. So, if you're curious, books with a sales rank of 3,622,000 or better would be in the top 10% of the category.

"So, what does that number really mean?" you may be wondering.

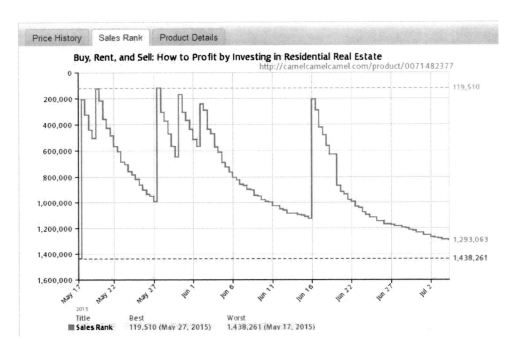

Figure 30

Here is the CamelCamelCamel.com sales rank information for the book, *Buy, Rent and Sell* by Robert Irwin (Figure 30), that's selling on Amazon. If you were to look up this book right now, either on Amazon.com or on your scanning device/app, you'd see that the current sales rank is 1,293,296 in Books. Not a bad rank, but let's spend some time looking at the graph above.

According to CCC, this particular book had its best sales rank of 119,510 on May 27, 2015, and had its worst rank on May 17, 2015 of 1,438,261. The longer that an item goes between sales, the worse the sale rank. On the graph above, there are six spikes in sales rank which, more than likely, correspond to sales. Every time a book sells, rank drops (in a good way) and then it slowly gets bigger until the next sale. So, according to this data, this particular book has sold 6 times in the last 2 months.

A Snapshot in Time

Sales rank is really, only a snap-shot in time. If you were out scanning books, and you came across a copy of this book on May 27th 2015, you may quickly come to the conclusion that this is a hot selling book. A book with a rank better than 120,000 would mean that this particular title is in the top .3% of books!

On the flip side, if you were to scan this book on May 17th 2015, you'd see that this book had a rank of 1,438,261 and would probably still buy it. But you wouldn't be as excited about it if you would have picked it up just 10 days prior. A rank of 1.5 million or better puts this book in the upper 4%.

How depressing would it be to buy this book on June 16th when the rank was at a very nice 200,000, thinking that it would sell right away? But as you can see by the data, that day was the last day that this listing had a sale.

Make Sure You're Asking the Right Question

Don't let the question, "Does this book have a good sales rank?" dictate your buying decision; instead as the question, "Does this book have a consistently good sales rank?" Meaning, not only do we want the book to have a decent sales rank, we want to see that the book has maintained that rank over time.

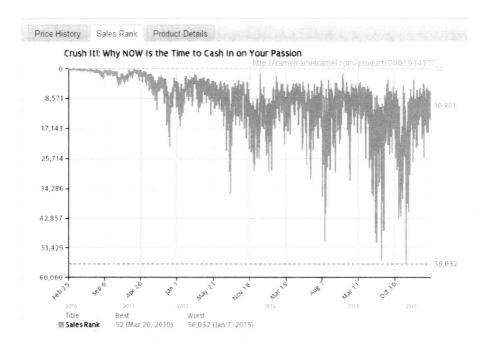

Figure 31

Here's the sales rank information for the book *Crush it!* by Gary Vaynerchuk (Figure 31). As you can see, since 2010, this book has maintained an Amazon Sales rank of 56,032 or better! That's the kind of rank consistency that we're looking for.

What's a Good Rank for a Book?

Remember, we are not only looking for a good rank, but a rank that is consistently good. We are looking for books that have, over the course of time, maintained their rank. Although this is still not a guarantee of a sale since past sales do not necessitate future sales, it is one piece of helpful information that could aid in making an educated buying decision.

In visiting the website www.fonerbooks.com, I came across some fascinating information regarding sales velocity by rank (Figure 32):

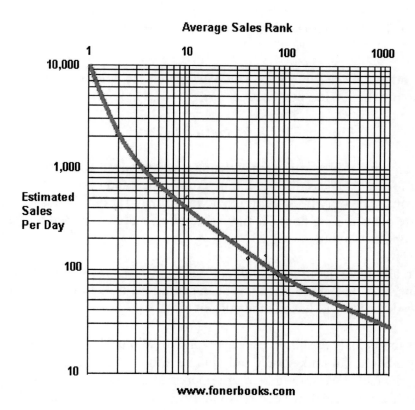

Figure 32

According to this chart, which roughly estimates sales per day based on Amazon's Sales Rank in the Book Category, I have come to these conclusions. We can anticipate that books that have a consistent rank will sell at this rate:

Sales rank of 1: 10,000 copies per day.
Sales rank of 10: 400 copies per day.
Sales rank of 100: 70 copies per day.
Sales rank of 1,000: 30 copies per day.
Sales rank of 5,000: 80 copies per day.

Sales rank of 10,000: 60 copies per day.
Sales rank of 100,000: 10 copies per day.
Sales rank of 300,000: 1.5 copies per day.
Sales rank of 500,000: 0.7 copies per day.
Sales rank of 1,000,000: 0.1 copies per day.

Keep in mind that these figures are rough estimates. Regardless, they should help put things into perspective.

Putting This Information to Work

Here's the problem. Since we are in a business where speed is the key, it's really hard for us to access historical rank consistency and scan books at 1-2 per second. The only information that we will have at our disposal when we are out scanning books is the information that is provided on the cell phone or PDA layout.

We won't really have the time to look up each item on CamelCamelCamel to determine if the particular book has been selling well over the last year or so. Instead, all we will have is the current rank.

My conclusion is that we should use sales rank to help us decide if we should buy a book, but rank should only play a minor role in our purchasing decision. We should be more interested in how much the book will cost us, for how much we can reasonably sell it on Amazon, and what our estimated net profit will be.

The Long Tail Book

Most online book sellers would probably admit that they would prefer to have their inventory filled with books that have a consistent Amazon rank of 100,000 or better. But, there is value in diversifying your inventory with best-selling, as well as, Long Tail books.

Authors and consumers alike can get caught up in the "Best Seller" buzz. Meaning, people can sometimes assume that the only way to succeed in the book business is to have a chart topping book. If our only focus is on selling the best of the best in the big general categories, we may be missing out on some good sales in the niche genres throughout the book selling world.

I am an online selling entrepreneur by trade, but when visiting my local Barnes and Noble, I can't find any books on my niche topic of choice. Honestly, If B&N carried the online selling books that I was looking for, I'd spend more money there. It's the same for my wife, but her niche of choice is "Home Birth." At the time this is written, Barnes and Nobles doesn't carry even a single book on the topic, why?

According to the CDC, there are about 35,000 recorded home-births in the U.S. every year, which represents about 0.7% of all births in the US. Although home births are increasing in popularity year-to-year, the trend still only represents a small segment of society. The home birth advocates are one niche group among thousands.

For the retailer, shelf-space is considered valuable real estate. Target, Wal-Mart, Best Buy, and Barnes and Nobles want to ensure that they are stocking their shelves with product that has the highest likelihood of selling. Since these retailers have an abundance of products to choose from, they have, for the most part, decided to play it safe and only carry those items that are the cream of the crop. They want to fill their shelves with products that have the highest likelihood of selling, and selling often. Unfortunately, little special interest niches are left by the wayside.

Chris Anderson, in his book *The Long Tail,* gives us some helpful information on the tip of the iceberg approach of modern retailers:

"More than 99 percent of music albums on the market today are not available in Wal-Mart. Of more than 200,000 films, TV shows, documentaries, and other videos that have been released commercially, the average Blockbuster carries just 3,000. Same for any other leading retailer and practically any other commodity – from books to kitchen fittings. The vast majority of products are not available at a store near you. By necessity, the economics of traditional, hit-driven retail limit choice"

That's crazy to me to think that retailers across the board only carry about 1% of all of the varieties that are in the world, whether it's books, movies, appliances, toys, or clothing.

Amazon Has Lowered the Cost of Connecting Supply and Demand

Amazon has given the consumer the ability to have more variety in their lives. As consumers, we are empowered to buy the things we want, regardless if they are mainstream items or not. The other 99 percent of the items that are created and sold, the ones that aren't stocked at your local big-box store, are marketable on Amazon.

So what does this mean for selling books? In the early 1990s, the book industry was booming and Barnes & Noble and Borders kept taking their businesses to the next level. These mega stores carried as many as 100,000 titles, which was five times more books than the average local bookstore. But, even if they carried 100,000 titles, they were still grossly misrepresenting all that was really out there. According to Forbes Magazine, there are somewhere between 600,000 to 1,000,000 books published every year in the U.S. alone. Jeff Bezo saw the opportunity and took it.

"So that became the idea: let Amazon.com be the first place where you can easily find and buy a million different books." Jeff Bezo quoted in the book *The Long Tail* by Chris Anderson.

Bezo was completely underestimating himself; now we find that the book category alone has over 36,000,000 million ranked titles for sale.

The Long Tail Defined

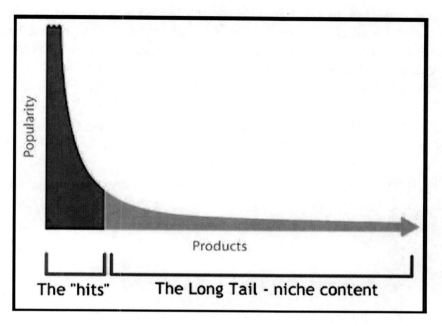

Figure 33

"The theory of the Long Tail can be boiled down to this: Our culture and economy are increasingly shifting away from a focus on a relatively small number of hits (mainstream products and markets) at the head of the demand curve, and moving toward a huge number of niches in the tail. In an era without the constraints of physical shelf space and other bottlenecks of distribution, narrowly targeted goods and services can be as economically attractive as mainstream fare" (Anderson, p.52).

The internet is driving people away from the hits and down the tail (Figure 33). This book, that you're reading right now, is just as accessible as a copy of <u>Harry Potter</u>. Customers are now making purchasing decisions based on keyword internet searches and are no longer restricted by retail shelf space and geography. The "Tail", which represents all of the books that are not considered "Hits", has really fattened up as a result of the power and technology that Bezo has put in the hands of his customers.

Anderson goes on to say, "Traditional retail economics dictate that stores only stock the likely hits, because shelf-space is expensive," but we find ourselves in a new frontier of online retail economics. Now on Amazon, we can find virtually everything in stock. Big wigs in multimillion dollar companies no longer choose what buying options we have. We do.

Some of our best sellers are the books that are VERY specific in their content.

Devil's Knot: The True Story of the West Memphis Three
ASIN: 0743417593
Product Dimensions: 9 X 6.1 X 1.4 inches
Shipping Weight: 1.45 pounds

See Product Details ⌧

Figure 34

Just today, we sold this book titled *Devil's Knot: The True Story of the West Memphis Three* (Figure 34). This is a non-fiction book on a very specific historical event in a small town in West Memphis Arkansas. That's pretty specific; we were obviously marketing this book to a specific niche of buyers.

Hou Hanru: On The Mid-Ground
ASIN: 9628638823
Product Dimensions: 8.52 X 6.24 X 0.93 inches
Shipping Weight: 1.38 pounds

See Product Details ⌧

Figure 35

Here's another "Long Tail" book that we sold earlier this afternoon (Figure 35). By looking at the sales rank, it is obviously not a "Hit". Once again, the subject matter had "I'm a Niche Book!" written all over it. Sometimes the more obscure the topic, the better.

 Culture Shock! Germany: A Survival Guide to Customs and Etiquette (Culture Shock! A Survival Guide to Customs & Etiquette)
ASIN: 1558689303
Product Dimensions: 8.11 X 4.96 X 0.79 inches
Shipping Weight: 0.84 pounds

See Product Details 🗗

Figure 36

This "Long Tail" book, *Culture Shock! Germany*(Figure 36) is another excellent example of how booksellers can make money focusing a good deal of their attention on "Long Tail" books, as opposed to only chasing after the Hits.

Now, don't go out there and buy every single obscure title that you come across. Be sure to make sure that it passes all of your other buying criteria. But, don't be afraid to give some Long Tail books a try. Let's say you come across a book like this one:

 **Shotgun Lovesongs (Thorndike Press Large Print Basic Series)**
ASIN: 1410470415
Product Dimensions: 8.5 X 5.5 X 1 inches
Shipping Weight: 1.4 pounds

See Product Details 🗗

Figure 37

If you could buy this book (Figure 37), *Shotgun Lovesongs* (I'm really not even sure what this book is about), for less than a couple of bucks, why not give it a try? I know that it has a sales rank of 4,000,000+ but there's not much FBA competition, the profit margin looks pretty nice.

Separating the Long Tail Studs from the Duds

Just because a book has a high rank and there are some sellers on the listing that have priced it high, that does not necessarily mean that it is a Long Tail book (a book with little demand, but demand non-the-less). There are books that have a poor sales rank that will never sell. They're not really Long Tail books, because all of their demand has faded away over time. These typically are books that were written on a topic that was once popular and/or useful, but are now obsolete. Here's an example:

 Microsoft Office 98 Macintosh Edition at a Glance (At a Glance (Microsoft))
ASIN: 157231916X
Product Dimensions: 9 X 7.2 X 0.8 inches
Shipping Weight: 1.2 pounds

Figure 38

This book on Microsoft Office 98 (Figure 38) has a rank of just over 11,000,000, and I would argue, even if the profitability looked good, pass on this one. This book is focused on outdated technology. The rank is more of an indication of no demand than the type of demand and cues that we look for in Long Tail books.

Finding the Quick Turn and Long Tail Balance

Books that are considered a "Quick Turn" are books that are expected to sell fast. (I think that the general consensus is that a book needs to have a consistent rank of 1,000,000 to fit into this category). To be honest, I would prefer that my inventory was filled with books that were expected to be sold within a month or less. The reality is that if I was determined to only find quick turning books, I would be leaving a lot of money on the table. So, the best approach to stocking an inventory of books is one in which you find a balance between books that you are sure will sell within a month or two and those that may take upwards of a year plus (Long Tail books are generally considered to be books with a consistent rank over 1,000,000).

As you begin to grow your inventory, you'll notice that mixed in with the better ranked, fast selling books will be long tail books. All I'm really concerned about is that a steady stream of long tail books sells month by month. I know that some will take years to sell, but the ones that are selling in the meantime will make it easier to be patient with the rest. The end result is that we sell high ranked, long tail books every day, and they have really become a staple in the profits that we bring in every week. I figure that our inventory, at any given moment, is comprised of about 60% quick turning books and 40% long tail books. This balance has done well to provide us with a consistent source of sales. Keep in mind that we didn't plan our inventory to shape up the way that it has; it has just naturally come together this way.

How to Determine Whether or Not a Task can be Outsource-able

When trying to decide which tasks or roles within your company are "outsource-able" it may be wise to consider the value of time. Think about it this way, when considering a task ask yourself the question, "If I were to pay someone to do this job how much would I have to pay them?" or "What is the market rate, per hour, for this particular kind of work?". Next, ask yourself the very important question, "Is my time worth that?"

When it came to picking, packing and shipping (for our Amazon business), which was currently taking up a considerable amount of my time every week, this was $10/hour work. I could probably hire a neighborhood high school age kid to do all of my fulfillment and I'm sure that they would be happy to do it for $10 an hour, don't you think? Because, I was willing to hustle and build a multifaceted online selling company that could support my family and provide good paying jobs I knew that my time was worth way more that $10/hour. So finding a way to outsource shipping was a no-brainer. But instead of hiring local help, utilizing Amazon fulfillment services seemed to be the best choice.

Before I quickly touch on the pros of selling FBA, I want to put something into perspective for you. Last month we sold 978 books, which amounts to about 140 books per week. Let's assume that to fulfill each order, we would need to spend 5 minutes, on average (to pick, pack, and ship to the customer). This would involve receiving the notification of the sale, the printing of the packing slip, boxing and weighing the book, printing out the shipping label, and then setting aside the book to be dropped off at the post office. The five minutes would also include the average amount of time handling all of the applicable customer service issue. Let's do the math: 140 books x 5 minutes = 700 minutes or 11 ½ hours of work per week on order fulfillment each week!

Now in all reality, in our Amazon business, we sold over 2,200 total items (books and non-books) last month (a non-Q4 month), if we were to apply the 5 minute average to all categories in our Amazon business we would have dedicated over 183 hours of work to order fulfillment, which translates to 45+ hours per week! I don't know about you, but when I got into the Amazon business I would not have wanted to dedicate that many hours per week to any aspect of the business let alone logistics, especially since the work could better be outsourced to Amazon. Point-blank, we would have never achieve the amount of success that we've achieved selling online if it wasn't for the outsourcing services offered by Amazon. We would probably be spending 20 hours per week sourcing products and 20 per week fulfilling orders, and sadly this would have easily cut our sales in half.

We have a finite amount of time every day, week, month and year. Do we want to spend it doing the tasks that can easily be outsourced to willing employees? 11 hours is way too much time for me to be packing and shipping boxes. I'd rather spend that time with my family or investing it in other areas of the business that will bring in a higher rate of return. Wouldn't you? Aren't you wired the same way that I am?

Without getting into too much detail, Amazon offers the best customer service and logistics the world has ever seen. They are able to get a book to an Amazon customer faster than I could ever dream of on my own. They have their intricate system of warehouses and their lightning quick fulfillment capabilities it gives us, the 3rd party seller, the tools and speed that can elevate our business to the next level.

My first recommendation is that you, from the get-go, outsource your logistics with Amazon FBA. Really, it's a no brainer. I know that there are some book sellers out there that have a business model that favors merchant fulfillment over FBA. These sellers are what many people call "penny-book sellers". They sell books online for a penny or two, charge their customers shipping (MF) and then out of the excess shipping money, they make their profit. Not a bad model, but it's just not mine. I'll get more into our book buying criteria in a bit but suffice to say, we look to buy books that we can sell for a minimum of $10.95 and if you adopt the same or similar criteria, then I wholeheartedly suggest that you think strongly about FBA.

As previously mentioned, not only does Amazon handle the fulfillment with FBA, but they also kindly store all of your books for you. We currently have over 16,000 books for sale at the Amazon warehouses. There is no way that we could keep all of those books here at home, without putting a serious damper on our living areas. Not to mention the horror to wake up to our little 2 year-old paging his way through our copy of _Frommer's Newfoundland and Labrador_ by Dawn Chafe (currently listed for $250+), that little rascal!

Recap:
Step#1 Acquire a Barcode Scanning Device
Step#2 Outsource With FBA

Step# 3 Establish Book Buying Criteria

"Strategy without tactics is the slowest route to victory. Tactics without strategy is the noise before defeat." - Sun Tsu, Ancient Chinese Military strategist

What's Your Strategy?

If you are going to have any success paying people to shop for you, you need to establish a very firm buying criteria. Your shopper has to be able to figure out whether or not he/she should buy a particular item with confidence, preferably without having to call and check with you first. The most difficult thing about coming up with an efficient and accurate buying criteria is that most business owners probably haven't taken the time to spell out that criteria for their business. When training our first few sourcing people, I really had to sit down and scrutinize our buying criteria which was great for helping us discover what we were really looking for. I needed to get that successful criteria out of my head and onto paper.

Don't be indispensable in this area of your company. Don't be the only guy/gal that has the key buying information locked in their head somewhere. The saying, "knowledge is power" is true. But, this is the type of power that if you hold onto it, you run the risk of missing out on huge scaling opportunities for your business.

So, spend some time outlining and sharpening your buying criteria. Run it through the ringer over and over again. When you finally decide to start bringing in buyers for your business, all this work that you have put in will pay off huge.

A quick definition of terms:

Book-Sourcer: This is someone who goes to the stores and sales to buy books for us. They are "Sourcing" books so from here on out I'll refer to these shoppers as "Book-Sourcers".
Book-Lister: This is someone who prepares, labels, packs and ships the books to Amazon for fulfillment.

Another thing worth mentioning is that you'll want to beef up your criteria a bit to accommodate the extra expenses associated with hiring people. These expenses include, but are not limited to, wages/commissions, extra equipment, and extra subscription fees for the operation of more scanning devices or selling apps. Before we completely outsourced our book-selling business, our criteria was different. Since we only had to cover the immediate costs of running a business and the rest of the earnings were ours to pocket, we were willing to buy books that had, on average, a lower sales cost. I will share with you our full buying criteria for our Book-Sourcers in a moment, but, where we used to buy books that we could potentially sell for $9.00 and now our minimum sales price is $10.95. We needed to make sure that the extra handful of dollars spent to pay for our outsourcing endeavors wouldn't completely erode all of the profitability of the company. Even with the sky-high margins in used books, it is worthwhile to sit down and crunch the numbers to ensure that you have a viable business strategy in regards to employee compensation.

Due to the straight forward nature of book sourcing, coming up with a solid, no gray area book sourcing criteria was pretty simple. Coming up with buying criteria for our retail shoppers was much more challenging. When I say 'retail shopping' I'm referring to the things that we buy at retail stores that are not books. With retail shopping, there are so many other variables to consider, which makes it much more difficult to hone in on sure fire criteria. Not to mention that the up-front investment in retail items is far greater than used books, having more money invested up front requires an extra level of diligence when evaluating product in the store. But, I digress. Retail sourcing criteria is a topic for another time perhaps.

Simplify Things

Here is a quick look at our book buying criteria. Our book sourcing people are trained in to adhere to these very simple standards:

- Only buy books for **$2.00 or less**.
- Only buy books that can be sold, in their current condition, for at least **$10.95.**
- Only by books with an **Amazon Sales Rank** of 1 – 5,000,000.

That's essentially it! It used to be way more complicated than that. We had a giant multi-row table that broke down acceptable selling prices based on buying cost and rank, but I think it was more confusing than helpful. Over the last year we have really simplified things. Here are some other things that we ask our Book-Sourcers to be mindful of:

- Make sure that the title of the book you are scanning **matches the title on the PDA**.
- Are there any pages missing?
- Is there excessive writing or highlighting? Does this obscure the text?
- Is the ethical nature of the book questionable?
- Is the book supposed to have a dust-jacket? Is it intact?
- Does the book promise any extras (DVD or CD)? Are they enclosed?
- Does the book come with an access code? Has it been opened, scratched or removed?
- Although **Amazon Rank** is typically overlooked here are a few things to consider:
- Is the poor rank a reflection of a lack of supply?
- Is the poor rank a reflection of a lack of FBA sellers?
- According to your good judgment, is this book outdated, and unlikely to sell?

How our Book-Sourcers answer these questions could further assist them in determining whether or not to buy the book. When we train our people we make sure to cover all of these questions and more to ensure that we're all on the same page. Since they have been equipped with a PDA, that's loaded with all of the pertinent information, such as sales rank and the going rate on Amazon (separated by condition), they will have all of the info they need to make accurate, split-second buying decisions.

What about the competition?

When sourcing for non-books it is usually a good idea to keep an eye on the number of offers. The more offers there are on a particular listing, the more competition you'll have, which means that if even only a couple of the Amazon sellers get an itch the price could quickly fall. When it comes to books, we tell our Book-Sourcers to disregard the number of other Amazon sellers, and instead focus on price. If they determine that we will be able to price our book competitively irrespective of the competition, they should buy it.

What About All of Those Penny Sellers!

You don't have to be scanning books for long to run across a ton of books that are selling on Amazon for $1 or less. In fact, depending on which book section that you're sourcing, you may not find any that could be bought and then re-sold for a profit. How frustrating would that be! Don't dismay. There are plenty of books out there that have incredible re-sale value. You just need to know where to find them.

To give you an example, we will look at a once popular fiction book. Fiction books generally don't have very good re-sale value. Typically, a mass produced title will be released, and for a brief period of time, the price will be high and then will inevitably drop. There are a couple of reasons why this happens. Fiction books are typically read only once, and as soon as some readers are finished, they rush to sell their copy on Amazon. Here is a snap-shot of the listing page for the book The Hunger Games (Figure 39):

The Hunger Games (Book 1)
ASIN: 0439023521
Product Dimensions: 8.4 X 5.2 X 1 inches
Shipping Weight: 0.75 pounds

See Product Details

Figure 39

This book was released in 2010 and Amazon is swarming with sellers looking to sell their used copies. Currently, you could buy a New copy for $6.21(FBA), or you could buy it Used starting at $0.01 from one of the 1984 offers! Obviously, there's more supply than there is demand, and prices have tanked accordingly. Let's take a closer look (Figure 40):

$3.99 *Prime*
+ $0.00 estimated tax

Used - Good

This item is gently used in good or better condition. If it is a textbook it may not have supplements. It may have some moder... » Read more

FULFILLMENT BY AMAZON ▾

- In Stock.
  - Free Two-day Shipping: Get it Wednesday, July 8.
  - Order within 52hr 14min for these delivery dates.
- Domestic shipping rates and return policy.

$3.99 *Prime*
+ $0.00 estimated tax

Used - Acceptable

This book has already been well loved by someone else and that love shows. It MIGHT have highlighting, underlining, be missin... » Read more

FULFILLMENT BY AMAZON ▾

- In Stock.
  - Free Two-day Shipping: Get it Wednesday, July 8 (order within 55hr 44min)
- Domestic shipping rates and return policy.

$3.99 *Prime*
+ $0.00 estimated tax

Used - Good

Solid used copy with visible wear to covers. May contain underlines or highlights. Ships directly to you with tracking from A... » Read more

FULFILLMENT BY AMAZON ▾

- In Stock.
  - Free Two-day Shipping: Get it Wednesday, July 8 (order within 54hr 44min)
- Domestic shipping rates and return policy.

$4.00 *Prime*
+ $0.00 estimated tax

Used - Good

Book has wear from being read. Possible creases to binding, underlining or highlighting. A good readable copy.

FULFILLMENT BY AMAZON ▾

- In Stock.
  - Free Two-day Shipping: Get it Wednesday, July 8 (order within 52hr 44min)
- Domestic shipping rates and return policy.

$0.01
+ $3.99 shipping
+ $0.00 estimated tax

Used - Good

We ship same or next business day. Small seller, big service. Book will be in good or better condition. Sorry, may

- In Stock.
- Expedited shipping available.
- Domestic shipping rates and return policy.

Here are the top five used offers priced from highest to lowest. As you can see, at the top of the list, there's an FBA seller who is selling their Used-Good copy for $3.84. Can they make any money selling it at that price? Let's head on over to the FBA Revenue Calculator to find out (Figure 41):

Revenue	Your Fulfillment	Amazon Fulfillment
Item Price	$ 0.00	$ 3.84
Shipping	$ 0.00	$ 0.00
Revenue Subtotal	$ 0.00	$ 3.84
Cost		
Amazon Referral Fee	$ 0.00	$ 0.58
Variable Closing Fee	$ 1.35	$ 1.35
Fulfillment Cost		
Order Handling	$ 0.00	$ 0.00
Pick & Pack	$ 0.00	$ 1.04
Outbound Shipping	$ 0.00	N/A
Weight Handling	$ 0.00	$ 0.63
30 Day Storage	$ 0.00	$ 0.01
Inbound Shipping	$ 0.00	$ 0.26
Customer Service	$ 0.00	Amazon Provided
Prep Service	$ 0.00	$ 0.00
Fulfillment Cost Subtotal	$ 0.00	$ 1.94
Cost Subtotal	$ -1.35	$ -3.87
Margin Impact	$ **-1.35**	$ -0.03

Figure 41

In the box on the top right, I entered the estimated sale price ($3.84) and estimated inbound shipping costs ($0.26), and as you can see, after all of the Amazon fees are collected, we would end up losing $0.03 on this book if we sold it at this price! This is not even taking into consideration the cost of the book and the time that would be spent preparing it for sale. Since we are trying to make a profit selling books, this particular book should be avoided. What about selling this book MF (Merchant Fulfilled)? If we sold and shipped the book directly to the customer, could we make a little money?

$0.01

+ $3.99 shipping
+ $0.00 estimated tax

Used - Good

We ship same or next business day. Small seller, big service. Book will be in good or better condition. Sorry, may not include access code or CD.

Figure 42

The cheapest MF seller is selling this book in Used – Very Good condition for $0.01 plus shipping (Figure 42). How can someone sell a book for $0.01 and make any sort of a profit!? They key is the money they collect for shipping, $3.99. Shipping this book via USPS Media Mail will probably cost about $2, which means that the seller stands to make about $2 before other costs and Amazon fees. On this particular book, Amazon charges a fee of $1.35. This would leave the seller with $.65 profit. They would also need to deduct any other costs associated with acquiring and processing this book, but as you can see, there is a small profit to be made. Online book sellers who sell in volume must have a system in place to make books like this worth selling.

There's another site, CamelCamelCamel.com, which provides some valuable insight about price and sales rank history for Amazon products. Here's what I discovered when I pulled up our Hunger Games book:

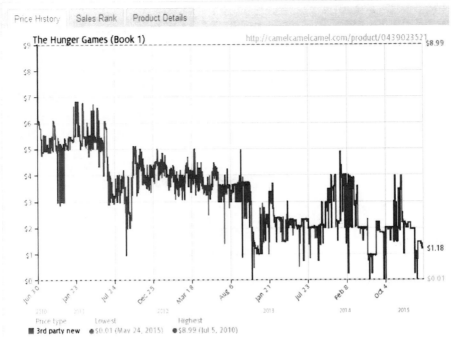

Figure 43

Just like I suspected, the price started high upon its release and then has slowly declined over the subsequent months (Figure 43). This is pretty typical for paperback fiction.

Don't assume that if a MF seller is selling the book for pennies that you should avoid it as a FBA seller. Make sure to also check the comparable FBA prices; sometimes, MF penny books can still be priced and sold for a nice profit via FBA.

All About Storage Fees

Amazon will charge storage fees for the inventory that you have stored at a fulfillment center, and these fees should be taken into consideration when establishing a book buying criteria. I know all of this information can seem rather overwhelming when you are just starting, but don't feel too overwhelmed.

Storage fees are charged for all units stored in an Amazon fulfillment center based on calendar month and your daily average volume (measured in cubic feet). The cubic feet of any unit will be based on the unit's size as properly packaged and ready for shipment to customers in accordance with the FBA Program Policies.

Short Term Storage Fees

There is some variation on fees from book to book, but this is what you can generally expect for Amazon storage fees:

$.01 per month for a trade paperback (or $.15/year)
$.03 per month for a textbook (or $.45/year)

Although these fees may be worth consideration, they shouldn't be the thing that deters you from selling on Amazon. In fact, Amazon's fees are very reasonable in my opinion, but they had to put some sort of fee structure in place, otherwise sellers may decide to use Amazon Fulfillment centers as personal storage facilities. At least, with these minimal fees, there is some incentive in place for sellers to sell.

One of the main reasons I don't allow Amazon storage fees to get me down is because there is no way in the world that I would be able to store my 15,000+ inventory of books at my house. No way!

Long Term Storage Fees

Here's what you need to know. You'll be charged an extra fee every six months for two reasons: 1) you have more than one copy of an item, and 2) you have it in storage for more than six months.

For all items that qualify, you'll be charged $22.50 per cubic foot. "What does $22.50 per cubic foot mean?" you may be wondering. This means a fee of about $1.10 for your average-sized paperback book. Again, this fee only comes into play when you have more than one copy of a book for sale at an Amazon fulfillment center, and it has been there for over 6 months. If you only have one book in stock, you will not be assessed this fee.

Just remember that one of the perks of selling books on Amazon is that they can have incredible profit margins, and one of the benefits of large profit margins is that they can accommodate these fees without a major impact on the bottom line.

In order to avoid long-term storage fees, although we hardly every run into this problem (having more than one copy of the same book in the same condition for over a year), we automatically set up our seller account to have extra units, which would otherwise incur fees, shipped back to us first. Here's how to set that up...

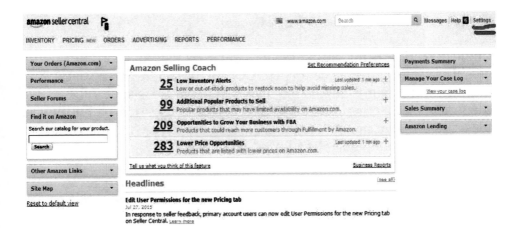

Figure 43

First, select the "Settings" Menu in the upper right-hand corner of the Amazon Seller Central homepage. From the drop-down menu, select "Fulfillment by Amazon" (Figure 44):

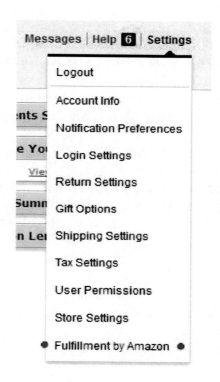

Figure 44

Once you get to the Fulfillment by Amazon settings page, you'll be able to set up automatic removal. Scroll down to "Automated Long-Term Storage Removals Settings" and choose the option "Return all units eligible for Long Term Storage Fee" and then be sure to fill out all of the pertinent shipping information (Figure 45). There is a fee per unit to have them removed; at the time of writing this it is $.50/book ($.50 for standard - sized units and $.60 of oversized units). If you'd prefer to just have the book destroyed, Amazon would be happy to do this for you for a fee of $.15/book.

Automated Long-Term Storage Removals Settings	
Automated Long-Term Storage Removals: Learn more	Return all units eligible for Long Term Storage Fee

Figure 45

While you're on this page, you might as well set up your account to automatically remove "unfulfillable" items. If a book is in transit, at the warehouse, or is returned damaged by a customer, and Amazon determines that this item is no longer sell-able, they will pull it from their website. This item will show up in your FBA inventory as "Unfulfillable". You really only have two options. You can: 1) have Amazon ship it back to you so that you can consider re-assessing its condition and re-sending it in, or you can have Amazon destroy it; the same fees mentioned above apply.

We opt to have our entire "unfulfillable" inventory automatically shipped back to us. Don't let this conversation scare you, though; it really is a very small percentage of our overall inventory that's deemed "Unfulfillable" or "Eligible for Long Term Storage Fees" but for the sake of cleaning house and avoiding any unnecessary fees, it's a good idea to have a good system like this in place.

Recap:
Step #1 Acquire a Scanning Device
Step #2 Outsource With FBA
Step #3 Establish Book-buying Criteria

Step #4 Locate and Research Local Thrift Stores

"By failing to prepare, you are preparing to fail."
-Benjamin Franklin

Prepare Your Business for Success

It is imperative for us to set up our employees up for success. We want to do everything possible to put our people in a winning situation. So, your people understand the buying criteria, have a fully loaded PDA in hand, and are ready to hit the road, but where do they go? How are we helping them find direction? How can we make sure that they are maximizing their time?

Just like with the buying criteria, we want to take all of the guess work out of shopping or working for our companies. There are people who think out of the box, and are creative and quick witted enough to figure things out on then fly, but the other 95% of people need a clear prescription of tasks otherwise they'll fail. With our people, we want to change the "lizard brain" mentality within that is so prevalent in our society today. Having a "lizard brain", a famous term coined by Seth Godin, essentially means that the individual lacks the ability to think for themselves. Instead of showing flashes of brilliance and discernment, these unfortunate minds typically won't make decisions based on logic, but instead are motivated more by group-thinking and fear. They would rather stick with what is safe and socially acceptable than take any risks. Conversely, we want the people who are working for us to see opportunities in areas that we don't see it. We want them to have drive and initiative. We want them to think like us, like forward-thinking, vision-minded entrepreneurs. We want the people in our company to use and embrace the unique gifts and strengths given to them by God. In fact, we are so serious about this that we work enrichment into some of our employee's schedules. I'm getting off track, but you'll read more on this later.

Whether it's retail stores, sales calls or thrift stores, give your people a hand by making them a map. Using Google Maps and a tool that came pre-loaded on my Windows computer called a Snipping Tool, I create a full color, detailed map with all the important locations marked and numbered. On the reverse side of the map, I print out a numbered list of all of the stores with addresses so that while my shoppers are traveling around town they will have some direction. They can familiarize themselves with the geography, the roads, towns, etc., or they can simply plug the addresses into the GPS on their phone.

Also, when I map out stores for them, I make sure to string them along, in the order of highest efficiency. I know that if one of my shopping people is going to be sourcing around in the metro area all day, they should definitely approach it systematically. I make sure that they hit the stores in order, say from East to West, as much as possible. Also, if they are going to drive downtown I determine a route to avoid any rush hour traffic at all costs. There's no need for having your shopper pushing through stop and go traffic if it can be avoided.

What Types of Books Should be Scanned?

If you ask 10 different booksellers, you may get 10 different answers. But usually, we are all in agreement that non-fiction is the best overall category to source books in. These are my favorite book categories in order:

1. Reference (textbooks)
2. Business
3. History
4. Biography
5. Religion
6. Arts and Crafts
7. Health
8. Travel

I encourage our Book-Sourcers to hit each of these sections in this order. But, if they want to venture into other sections, they are more than welcome to. In fact, we just sold a handful of Children's books, although we usually don't have much luck in that section.

Selling Textbooks via FBA

My favorite time of the year is late August through January. Why? Because it is bookselling season, and the books that typically sell the best and for the most amount of profit are textbooks. Class is in session in colleges throughout the country. Students are looking for a cheaper alternative for their required reading and often turn to Amazon for the solution. Whether they are looking for a good deal or someone who can get them their book ASAP, our Amazon business provides the solution to both of those problems.

Selling FBA means that your scholarly customers can rest assured that their books will be delivered on time, right when they need them. Also, Amazon has a Student Program that gives college and university students free shipping for six months (as long as you have an active .edu email address).

There is a clear advantage to selling textbooks FBA vs. MF, and it is a guaranteed speed of delivery. Time and time again, people will spend way more for an FBA copy over the MF comparable just because they need it to be delivered fast.

Next, we are going to talk about strategy and about the places that I think are best for Book-sourcing:

1. Thrift Stores

Thrift stores are our most reliable source of inventory. They are far more predictable and regular than the other options. If you know how to work the sales, they can also offer books at or below the $2 minimum purchase price, which is what you will be on the lookout for. I'll get into library book sales in a bit, but one advantage to thrift stores, over library sales is that if you go during the week and during the day, you won't have to fight crowds. I'm an introvert. I would much rather scan books without people looking over my shoulder or getting in my way. If your shoppers are wired the same way, they will appreciate the less competitive nature of a thrift store.

Which Thrift Stores?

Okay, so I talked you into putting together a map and that's great. But, which stores and locations are you going to put on it? You know you need to send them somewhere, but where? We create a map for each different thrift-store chain in your area. So, we have a map of all of the metro area Goodwill stores, a map of all the area Savers and Unique stores, a map of all of the Salvation Army Thrift stores, a map of all of the Valu-villages, and a "best of the rest" store map. If you haven't already, you should really familiarize yourself with what sourcing opportunities are in your area, and then type them up and print them out. Google search "Thrift Store" and drive around town. Some thrift stores don't have a website, and/or they haven't positioned themselves online very well and it would be hard to find them by searching Google. Don't leave any stone unturned!

Typically, people who have worked "normal" jobs their whole life may find it difficult, at first, to do more than you ask of them. Someone who has been an exchangeable cog in someone's factory or business their whole life is used to their bosses telling them exactly what they need to do. Thinking for themselves and thinking outside of the box is often discouraged. I was there once, I know! So, at least in the beginning, spoon-feed them as much as you can. Set them up for success, and make it so that they don't have to do much thinking. Once you have invested in them, and enriched their minds to the possibilities that are out there, then you can encourage them to branch out and find opportunities that you haven't discovered yourself.

Document Reoccurring Thrift Store Sale Days

Next, we need to figure out when to send them to these stores. Familiarize yourself with the various reoccurring sales and discounts that your list of stores offer throughout the week. The book prices at some of our local Goodwill stores can be frustratingly high, but did you know that on certain days of the week they discount certain tag colors? Why not have your shoppers hit the stores on these days and specifically look for these colored tags? Your only opportunity to gather up inventory that meets your criteria may be on these sale days.

Also, many thrift-stores offer discounts for people who donate. At Savers (a thrift-store in the mid-west) they give you a 20% off coupon when you donate two bags or more, and this coupon can be used towards inventory. Sticking with Savers, all stores have an offer "Buy 4 books, Get 1 Free". When we take advantage of this deal coupled with a freshly earned 20%

off coupon, we're well on the way to helping our shoppers hit their $2 per book maximum buying price.

Call or visit all of the stores in your area and write down which days they have sales and what kind of discounts your shoppers can expect. Beyond the weekly sales and discounts that they offer, ask them for the details of any other sales that they have throughout the year, such as Presidents Day and Martin Luther King Jr. Day. It may be a good idea to put these in on a monthly calendar to give to your Book-Sourcers.

Talk to Management

Books can be a thrift store's worse nightmare. A typical store will have shelves and shelves of books on the sales floor but may also have an equal amount or more books in the back waiting to be shelved. Our local store has to move the entire book section, across the store, several times a year! Usually the books are displayed up front but for Halloween and Christmas they are relocated to the back of the store. Don't you think that these thrift store managers want these books to sell? You may be their only opportunity to unload all of their pretty obscure titles.

I would highly recommend that you schedule a brief appointment with the store manager to see if they would be willing to give you a discount for making a bulk purchase. If you're not sure what to say, say something along the lines of, "I'm planning on buying over 100 books today and I was wondering if you would be willing to offer me an additional discount for buying such a large amount?" They may only offer you an additional 10-20% off, but it's worth it right?

Andrew, our book-selling manager, asked this very question to the manager of a small Christian books store in the cities and he was quickly ushered into the backroom. The manager said that they have more books than they had room out front and that he was welcome to scan the shelves in the back. He was also extended an additional 20% off, which is fantastic!

Don't Thrift Stores Sell Books Online Now?

This objection to thrift-store sourcing comes up from time to time and it's worth considering. There are some Goodwill stores that scan books in the back and then pick the good ones out to be sold online. Although this isn't good news for us online book-sellers, don't let it discourage you too much. This is why, Goodwill sells books on Amazon and Merchant Fulfills them. This means that books that would be a profitable FBA selection, but not a good MF sell, will be overlooked.

Time and time again, we scan a book that is selling Merchant Fulfilled for only a couple of dollars plus shipping ($3.99). This would cost the customer $5.99 and would probably be a book that the thrift-store would skip. But, that same book could be sold by a Fulfillment by Amazon seller, in the same condition, for $10.95+. For $5.99, the Amazon customer would get the book that they wanted in the condition that they wanted from this third-party seller (MF). But they would have no guarantee of when it would arrive and they would have the added anxiety of knowing that they would have to deal with this little, possibly stubborn book-seller, if things went wrong. The allure of having guaranteed 2-day shipping plus the promise of being able to work with Amazon directly if returns need to be made often motivate people to spend extra money on a book that is Prime Eligible (or FBA'd) rather than buying a much cheaper book that's Merchant Fulfilled.

I once sold a book for $24.95 FBA, and the very same book in the very same condition was being sold MF for only $8.95. This means that the customer valued the expedited shipping and the promise to work with Amazon directly, if there was a problem, so much that they were willing to pay over $15 more for the same book! This is not an irregular occurrence.

2. Books Sales

Library sales are a great place to find cheap books. Depending on which sales you go to, they can be a bit more crowded. But if you don't mind navigating your way through the narrow aisles of a sale, then you will be very pleased. On average, the books that we source at library sales are acquired for less than a dollar, and if you hit a library sale on their last day often times you can buy books at less than fifty cents per piece. This is much cheaper than the prices that most thrift stores have to offer. Also, the sheer volume of books that you can source can make even your best thrift store look pathetic. One of our part time book sourcing people was able to source over 100 books in 1 hour at a local bi-annual library sale last week. This type of volume in that amount of time is typically abnormal when sourcing in stores.

You should be on the look of for national and local books sales, both will offer you a big opportunity to find a bunch of new inventory:

National Sales

If you haven't already, you should swing over to www.booksalefinder.com to check out their list of national book sale events that are taking place this year. Just like any other book source, there are pros and cons to national book sale events.

The Pros: National sales events usually sell a ton of books. One year, we traveled to St. Louis to attend the million+ book YMCA sale, and the amount of books that they had was insane. I literally had to spend two full days of scanning just to be able to get through all of the non-fiction sections. We sourced over 700 books on that trip, and we prepped and shipped them out of the hotel room the next day, which was pretty sweet! Every major city seems to have book sales published on this site, which would make it very easy for you to plan out a trip for one of your Book-Sourcers.

Do you have friends or family that need a job? Would they like to travel all around the U.S. making great money in the process? Think about the opportunities!

The Cons: There are draw-backs to these heavily advertised national sales events. Every other book seller in the country knows that they exist and if the sale is big enough, it will likely garner the attention of book sellers across the nation. At the YMCA sale, I arrived at the sale at 5am in the morning to wait in line. The doors opened at 9am and we arrived early in order to be given a ticket that held our place in line for the sale, which started in the afternoon. Suffice to say, I was number 42. Everyone in front of me and the hundred or so people behind me were all book sellers, with scanners in hand, ready to hit the stacks. It was actually pretty exciting, even though I would rather send my Book-Sourcers to sales that had a little less competition.

I'm not trying to spoil national sales for you, I just want to give you a heads up to the seriousness some other sellers take these events. I was standing in line with a couple of gals from Colorado, at another national sale, and we got to talking. They sold children's books on eBay, and the lady in front of me sold antique books. Neither of them were looking for the same books that I was be looking for. Even if there were some other Amazon sellers there, are they selling FBA? What is their minimum allowable sales price? Are they lazy scanners? Do they skip books that don't look good?

There is a local book seller (he owns his own Amazon selling business) here in my home town whom I know well. He only buys books that he can sell for at least $25 and they have to have rank of less than 1,000,000. Typically, he would go to a store that would net us over a hundred books on a bi-weekly basis but he would only find 4 or 5. His criteria, in my opinion, is way too stringent. He's leaving way to many books on the shelf. Also, the amount of time that he's spending to find only 4 or 5 books would be maddening to me.

Local Sales

Book sales that tout 100,000 books or less tend to be ignored by the hoards of book-sellers, and these are usually the best! Some of these sales are advertised on the BookSaleFinder.com website, but others you'll have to do some digging to find. Start contacting local libraries, or have your shoppers call, with a pen and paper handy. Ask them when they have sales, how much they charge (to get in and per book), whether or not they have a preview night and if they allow "scanners".

For local sales we try to go to the preview night, if there is one, and then also on the last day. Most library sales finish off with a Bag Sale Day. For some of our sales, that means that each bag full of books only costs $5, instead of the typical $1-2 per copy. Our local libraries organize by county, so 4 or 5 locations will collaborate and have a sale together at one location quarterly or bi-annually. It's good to put in the work to find these sort of things out.

What is a "Preview Night"

Most book sales will open their doors early for their book buying customers that would like to shop before the doors officially the following day. If it's a Friends of the Library run sale, there is usually a fee that must be paid at the door prior to admittance. Also, these special sale events only last an hour or two. The benefits of having your Book-Sourcers go to the preview sale is that they will have first crack at the books before it is open to the general public. If there is any competition in town, you'll be able to at least have a fighting chance at the good books! I recommend that you have your Book-Sourcers go to both the preview night and the bag sale at the end of the week. It's good to take advantage of both of these opportunities.

What Does it Mean if a Sale Doesn't Allow "Scanners"?

Some sales that you find online will say something like "no scanners allowed" in the fine print, what does this mean? Great question! Unfortunately there are some bad apples out there that have given book-scanners a bad name. In the name of finding the most amount of profitable books as fast as possible, they tear up a book sale which completely ruins the sale for those who are organizing it and those who are attending it. I have heard stories of people with scanners grabbing books out of their sections by the handfuls huddling with them in corners, to scan through them quickly, only to leave the discarded books in a pile somewhere. Other, rude book-scanners have thrown blankets or tarps over entire sections to prevent other shoppers from looking at those books until they have had the time to scan through them. This behavior is discouraged by book sale operators, and it should be!

Unfortunately, some of these sales have come to the conclusion that the only way to eliminate this sort of behavior is to ban all "scanners". If you've found a sale that states "no scanners" give them a call or stop by and plead your case. Tell them that you will be very respectful of the other shoppers around you and that you promise to leave the books tables in better condition than you found them. They may make an exception! When training our Book-Sourcers, we encourage them to be the most courteous shopper the book section has ever seen. It makes for a good business relationship with the store of the sale workers if you clean and organize as you go. It's these little things that can assist you in forming some lucrative partnerships.

3. Other Places to Find Books

While it's true that the first two sources for books account for the bulk majority of our inventory, there are other sources to consider.

Estate Sales

There are several estate sale websites that may be worth you or your Book-Sourcer's time to sift through occasionally. If the sale advertises a large number of non-fiction books for sale, it may be worth sending someone there to shop. Be sure to call the company that is having the sale and ask them 1) How many books the sale will have 2) How much they will cost per title and, 3) Would they be willing to give you a discount if you bought a very large number of their books?

Garage and Rummage Sales

Garage, yard and rummage sales can be great places to find books. Just like with estate sales, it's important to check before hand if they have any books for sale and what they plan on charging per title. Garage and yard sales typically have the cheapest books but sometimes the selection lacks. It's good to plan ahead. Does your town have a city-wide garage sale day in the summer? It would be much easier to go quickly, from house to house scouting for books than it would be to drive all around town to hit up only a couple of sales. Again, efficiency is the key.

Recycle Centers

Books that are on their last leg are shipped off to a recycle center for disposal. Generally, books need to be de-bound before the paper can be recycled due to the glue in the binding. You should contact your local recycling center and ask them if they ever get books in that they have no idea what to do with. You may be able to score some free inventory!

Universities and Colleges

Put up fliers around universities and colleges. Simply draw up a one-page flier, offering to buy large quantities of non-fiction books. The main target, believe it or not, is faculty or students. Here's where the opportunities lie; we are looking to help professors unload any unneeded books. What professor doesn't have shelves and shelves of books at home or in their office that they need to get rid of? When you are trying to decide where to put your fliers, make sure that you have the professor in mind. Also, make sure to adhere to any campus rules about posting such advertisements.

Used Bookstores

Many online booksellers stay away from bookstores, because they assume that the bookstore will know the online value of their books, but don't think this way! Pricing a book is such a subjective practice. Since most online booksellers don't sell their books via FBA, they're probably already undervaluing their inventory. The only downfall of buying books at a Used Book store is that they generally cost more per title, but in exchange, the expected return is much greater.

Dumpster Sourcing

Most Book Sourcers choose to avoid this, sometimes very profitable, source for books. You want to be on the lookout for a place that throws away a lot of books. There are libraries, schools, and bookstores that have no idea what to do with their leftover books, and instead of donating them to the local thrift-store, they just dump them, in bulk, into their dumpster! I was sitting out front of my local library a few months ago, waiting for my wife and kids to come out, and I saw one of the friendly librarians. In her arms, she was carrying an armful of books; to my amazement, she walked over to the dumpster and proceeded to toss all of these books away! Go to a library in an upscale side of town, and see what you can find. Trust me;

it could be well worth your time!

Search Craigslist

When on Craigslist.com, search using the keywords "Books" and "Lot". Be on the lookout for large lots of books being sold, not the single booksellers (not worth your time). Occasionally, you'll find a bookseller who is going out of business and would like to sell their entire inventory. This can be an excellent opportunity to source high value books for pennies on the dollar.

University Surplus

Google search any large universities in your area and the word "Surplus" and see the search results. You're hoping to find out what this institution does with all of their extra books. If it's a decent sized school, they will have lots of them. The top three ways that a school will liquidate its surplus are: on campus surplus store, online auction, or standard auction. There are surplus stores with thousands of books that have gone untouched by our competition. Check out UnisversitySurplus.com to get an idea of what I'm saying.

Ebay

On eBay.com, search for large lots of books (500+). Typically, lots of books this size will be for pickup only, which is great, because it eliminates a lot of your online competition. Search your location and identify people selling large quantities of books in your area.

Yard Sales

These can be hit or miss, especially if you show up without doing some research first. Make sure to call or email the seller and ask them: 1) what types of books they are selling, and 2) how many they have. If you come upon a yard sale that has a nice selection of books that would interest you, suggest offering to "take them all."They are probably very motivated to sell and will likely give you a good deal. Sites worth checking are yardsales.net and garagesalestracker.com.

Auctions

Auctions happen for a variety of reasons, but typically, people rarely show up to bid on books. If you find a sale with a decent amount of books, you could very well come away with an excellent haul. Be sure to look around your local area and periodically check these sites;

Liquidation.com

This is one of the best online liquidation websites. Oftentimes, you can find some very interesting book offers.

Figure 46

Here's an example of a lot of textbooks that are currently being sold on this website (Figure 46). The highest bidder on this auction that ends today will get 23 textbooks (which you can evaluate online) with an estimated MSRP of $2,022. Currently, there are 13 bidders who have brought the bid up to $190.00.

Figure 47

This auction for "media items" is interesting. You could, potentially, get 133 items for less than $1/each. It may be worth checking out the manifest (the detailed list of the contents of this auction).

	Textbooks and Various Other Topics - Fully Manifested	Used	Brittreed	91	$100.00	0	Illinois	07/28/2015 03:55 PM	
	☐ Compare								
	Keyword found in Manifest								

Figure 48

Just as I was about to leave the site, this listing caught my eye. There were 91 textbooks starting at $100; that's just over $1/book. If they check out, we could have just stumbled upon a goldmine!

Put "Books" in the search box at the top of the page and see what you find. You may never order anything from these websites, but if you check periodically, you may come across the auction of all auctions, so it's worth checking from time-to-time!

Govdeals.com

GovDeals provides a service to a number of government agencies that allows them to sell surplus and confiscated items, typically in bulk, on the internet. Here are some of the results I got after searching for "Books" (Figure 49):

Books "Text & Reference"(07215-001) ID: 07215-001	Atlanta, GA	7/29/2015 10:45 AM ET	$2,000.00 Bids: 1
Books "Soft Back"(07215-006) ID: 07215-006	Atlanta, GA	7/29/2015 10:00 AM ET	$2,000.00
Books "Soft Back"(07215-007) ID: 07215-007	Atlanta, GA	7/29/2015 10:03 AM ET	$2,000.00
Books "Text & Reference"(07215-008) ID: 07215-008	Atlanta, GA	7/29/2015 10:48 AM ET	$2,000.00 Bids: 1
Books "Hard Back"(07215-009) ID: 07215-009	Atlanta, GA	7/29/2015 9:03 AM ET	$2,000.00

Figure 49

These lots of books, as pictured above, are being sold in giant "gaylords", which is a giant, triple-walled, corrugated pallet box. The only challenge you'll face is how to pick up these massive lots. If you could solve that problem, you could uncover some very profitable inventory.

Google Search

My recommendation is to Google search "Auction + your city" to find auctions in your area. Most local auction companies have their own websites now, and you'll typically be able to get a sneak peak at the auction before it opens. If you find a sale that has a lot of books for sale, you may want to attend.

Conclusion

I'm sure that I'm missing at least a couple of good sources for books, but I've covered the best ones. Be on the lookout for other opportunities. Be sure not to leave any stone unturned. Hopefully you've gained some value from this section, even if you have no ambition to sell books. Whether you're sending your employees to books stores, retail stores or on sales calls, the key is to put them in the position to succeed. Help them to, at least initially, focus fully on the main task, whether its scanning books, or selling products and services while you organize all of the logistics. I would rather have my new employees exert all of his or her energy on the main task and get a taste of true success than have them be too mindful of all of the details of running then ins and outs of the business and ultimately fail, or get mediocre results. So, now that you have the buying criteria in place and you have a geographical strategy for your people to plug into, now we need to determine the best way to compensate them for their hard work.

Step #1 Acquire a Barcode Scanner
Step #2 Outsource With FBA
Step #3 Establish Book-buying Criteria
Step #4 Locate and Research Local Thrift-stores

Step #5 Start Scanning

"Here's the deal. If you want it badly enough, the money is there, the success is there, and the fulfillment is there. All you have to do is take it. So quit whining, quit crying, and quit with the excuses."
-Gary Vaynerchuk from his book *Crush It!*

Time to Hit the Shelves!

Now that you've acquired a barcode scanner, established your buying criteria and have spent some time finding and researching local thrift-stores, I recommend that you get out there and do some scanning yourself! Book scanning can be lots of fun. You work your way down the shelves searching for profitable books, and when you finally do discover one it's quite the rush. Some people think that sourcing is sort of like looking for treasure. Imagine you're a pirate looking for gold!

The thought that gets me most excited is thinking about all of those profitable books that are just sitting there on a thrift-store or library sale book shelf, waiting to be sourced and re-sold. Before, it was impossible to determine, at a reasonable pace, whether or not a book is worth reselling, but now with technology this can be determined very quickly.

If you are having problems visualizing what books-scanning with a PDA looks like, check out this introductory video (if you haven't already):

https://www.youtube.com/watch?v=xOUH3VkTiGc

The reason why I recommend doing some sourcing yourself, before paying someone else to do it is: 1) It's easier to teach someone how to do something if you've already done it yourself, and 2) The excitement that you've experienced sourcing books is contagious.

Lead by Example

I'm not recommending that you need to become an expert book scanner, but having a basic grasp on the skill is really helpful when training your first Book-Sourcer. What typically happens when you hire someone to do a specific job is that after a short period of time, they will become proficient at it. In fact, if the people that you hire have top-talent (more on this in Step #8) they should be able to focus in on book-sourcing and be better at it than you ever could be. Let me give you an example. For several years, I sourced for all of our books myself. At least once or twice every week I would spend a day sourcing books at local book sales and thrift-stores, but sourcing the books wasn't all that I did. We also sourced games, movies, toys, and other electronics while at the thrift-stores, and it didn't take long for us to move out of the thrift-store and into retail stores. As I continued to grow our online selling business, my attention was obviously divided. Not to mention that fact that along with Book-Sourcing, I was also prepping, labeling and shipping all of the books of to Amazon myself, as well as managing and maintaining my online selling account.

As a multifaceted online selling company, there were a lot of plates to keep spinning.

When we trained Andrew to be our first Book-Sourcer, I already had several years and thousands of books worth of experience under my belt. In my mind, it was probably going to take him at least a year or possibly even more to achieve the level of expertise that I had. Well, I was wrong because Andrew's attention was focused solely on Book-Sourcing so he excelled at an astonishing rate. Within, literally, three weeks of serious, part-time sourcing, he was already doing better than I had done with my collective experience. The volume and quality of books he was purchases completely exceeded expectations.

Part of this success may have been due to the fact that we put him in a position to succeed, but the main reason for his success, I believe, is that he could focus on one thing, sourcing books. Don't get caught in the mindset that no one, but yourself, can do a specific task in your business. It's a trap! Watching our company expand by giving away outsource-able tasks has been exciting. It's been fun to watch Andrew and other members of our team, grow into their positions. Fast forward 6 months and Andrew is still growing and expanding the business not only as a Book-Sourcer, but also as our Book Sales Manager (I'll speak more about this in Step #8).

Your Excitement for Book-sourcing will be Contagious

It's fun to scan through a bookshelf and to find a book that truly exceeds the buying criteria. When I was training Matt, we found some excellent titles that we determined, based on the data, could be sold for $100+. You should have seen the excited looks on our faces as we quickly placed these high-dollar books in the cart. If they see you having fun and getting excited, then they will be encouraged to have fun too. Hopefully, when they find an excellent book they too will rejoice in their small victory. This should help them approach book sourcing with a fresh and positive perspective, which is best for all parties involved.

The more book sourcing that you do, the better you will be able to prepare those who you hire. You need to familiarize yourself with the stores, their sales, where they keep the best books, how to handle the cashier and other shoppers questions, to how to organize a full shopping cart of books, or how to efficiently pack a trunk. These things will all be helpful, when you give these tidbits of knowledge that your people will appreciate.

Don't Over Look the Value that You Provide in this Business

Often times books in this environment, are on their last legs. If they hit the library sale or thrift-store and they still can't find a new permanent home, then unfortunately they will more than likely end up in a landfill. Books are very difficult to recycle due to the glue on the binding, so unless your local recycle center has a book de-binder, which most don't, off to the garbage they go. Many of the books that we source are hard-to-find, out-of-print books, and this is why people are happy to pay well over MSRP for them. Think about it. Our wonderful Amazon customers are looking high and low for a particular book but they can't find it anywhere. When they look up the listing on Amazon, they are pleased to discover that you, a 3rd party merchant, are selling a gently used copy of the book that their dying to get.

We have the privilege of doing the hard work of sourcing, prepping and shipping these books into Amazon so that they can be listed for grateful customers to buy. Even though we sell way more items in other categories and not just books on Amazon, we still get more positive seller feedback from our book buyers than in any other category. We book sellers provide a great service. We take books that are seemingly destined for destruction, rescuing them and putting them in the hands of someone who wants them. Not only is book selling great for the environment, but it's good business!

If you would like to see a step-by-step visual of the Book-Sourcing

process go to this link to check out the thrift-store shopping Flow Chart that I put together:
http://profitsourcing.com/blog/thrift-store-sourcing-flow-chart

Step #1 Acquire a Barcode Scanner
Step #2 Outsource With FBA
Step #3 Establish Book-buying Criteria
Step #4 Locate and Research Local Thrift-stores
Step #5 Do Some Scanning Yourself

Step #6 Prepare, Label, Ship and Document

"I like thinking big. I always have. To me it's very simple. If you're going to be thinking anyway, you might as well think big. Most people think small, because most people are afraid of success, afraid of making decisions, afraid of winning. And that gives people like me a great advantage."
Donald Trump, from his book: *TRUMP: The Art of the Deal.*

Logistics

Now that the books have been purchased, how will you get them off to their next destination, the Amazon Fulfillment Center? Step #6 will cover the basics of what's necessary to prep, label and ship your books to Amazon. Not only is it important for you to familiarize yourself with the prepping and shipping process, it is also helpful if you document this process step-by-step so that you can teach someone else how to do this for you with ease. First, let's talk about equipment and supplies that you'll need to get started.

Supplies Needed to get Started

Here's a list of items that I recommend that you buy with their current prices. Be advised that prices may vary depending on your location. I just wanted to give you a good estimate of what it will cost to get things set up:

- **Heat Gun** $20 – This is for heating up stickers so that they can be removed. Some thrift-stores put giant, very sticky price tags and barcodes on their books. It's important to remove these before sending them in to Amazon. A focused heating element will help loosen up the adhesive and make it easier to remove the sticker without ruining the book. You can use a hair dryer although a heat gun, or embossing gun will work best.
- **Scotty Peelers** or **Plastic Razor Blades** $9 – Once the sticker has been heated up, it's nice to have a tool to help scrape it off.
- **Rubbing Alcohol** $3 – After the stickers have been heated up and scraped off, any remaining residue should come off with a little rubbing alcohol on a paper towel. Also, rubbing alcohol works great to clean up the cover of the books too.
- **USB Barcode Scanner** $25 – Unless you want to enter in each UPC/ISBN number in by hand then you will need some sort of USB barcode scanner. The one that we use plugs right into our USB slot in the front of our computer and works great!
- **30 White Address-sized Labels** $38 – Once a book has been listed, prior to shipping, Amazon will want you to print a white barcode to put on the book. These labels will have unique information that

will let Amazon know which specific book it is and who's book it is once it hits the fulfillment center. You can buy Avery Labels (white, 30 per sheet) at any office supply store. I order my labels off of Amazon from a company called House Labels for $38. You get 400 sheets or 12,000 which is a great deal.

- **Medium-sized Boxes** $1.10 each – Amazon requires that boxes shipped to their fulfillment centers weigh 50 pounds or less. Small-sized boxes from Home Depot or Uline work best. Your goal will be to tightly pack these boxes full of books and to get as close to the 50 pound mark as possible.

- **Brown Paper** $14/roll – After tightly packing a box, if there's still room you will need to fill in the gaps. We used to collect plastic shopping bags, fill them with crumpled newspaper, tie them shut and use this free solution for bunting. This is what they call material to fill in gaps. If you would rather spend a little money to go the more efficient route I suggest you buy some brown craft/shipping paper. We buy our giant rolls from Uline (go to www.Uline.com for prices).

- **Packing Tape** $2/roll – You'll need tape to seal your boxes of books. We use Scotch brand moving tape, which can be purchased in a 4-pack for about $2/roll. There are less expensive options out there for tape, but over the years I have determined that Scotch brand tape for this purpose is the best. Cheap tape won't stick to the boxes very well, which is very concerning to us. We would assemble a shipment and get it ready for UPS pick up the next day and notice that all of the tape is pulling away from the box. The last thing that we want is our box of expensive books to be all over the UPS truck floor! Also with Scotch tape, we can use about half the amount and feel confident that it will hold, there isn't a need to use the cheaper stuff.

- **Shipping Scale** $25 – before shipping your boxes of books off to Amazon you'll need to weigh them. We buy our 200lb max. digital scales at Sam's club.

- **Markers or Sharpies** $1 – These may be helpful as you are weighing boxes. I weigh each box and then write on the top of the box how much it weighs so that I don't forget later.

- **UPS Shipping Labels** FREE – You can order free shipping labels from UPS.com (a full sheet of paper with 2 large labels for your

UPS shipment) after you set up a shipping account with them. (I'll talk more about setting up a UPS account in a bit.)

- **HP DeskJet Printer** $30 – If you don't have a printer you'll need to buy one. You can buy HP printers at Wal-Mart for around $30.
- **Black and White Ink for a Printer** $6/each – We buy our replacement ink cartridges on Amazon. To save money, we buy the re-furbished cartridges at about $6 a piece.

Now that you have all of the necessary supplies, we will now look at a book listing program that I highly recommend that you consider. But before we do, I just want to make it clear that even if you're not interested in selling books on Amazon, it's a good idea to calculate all of your supply and equipment costs. When outsourcing, it's very important to consider all of the additional expenses that you will have when hiring a new employee. Having a list of expenses, such as this will help you determine whether or not adding an employees is worth it, and/or will help you more accurately estimate the profitability of the arrangement.

Invest in Book Listing Software

You could list all of your books on the Amazon Seller Central, but I feel like it's way too time consuming. Consider purchasing a program called Scanlister to make the listing process far more efficient. Also, with Scanlister I can have my Book-Lister, list books without having to worry about picking the correct price. As I'm writing this ScanLister, a program by Nathan Holmquist, will only cost you a one-time payment of $97. For more information on Scanlister visit www.scanlister.com.

All my Book-Lister has to do is while he or she is prepping the books is organize them in piles by condition. So, he or she will have a pile of books that are determined to be in New, Like-New, Very Good, Good and Acceptable condition. Next Book-Lister can use the program to list all of the books, by condition, at a very fast rate. He scans the barcode on the back of the book with the USB Scanner, and the UPC is immediately populated on the screen (more on this in a moment).

Here are Amazon's official condition guidelines for books:

- *New*: A brand-new, unused, unread copy in perfect condition. The dust cover and original protective wrapping, if any, is intact. All supplementary materials are included and all access codes for electronic material, if applicable, are valid and/or in working condition.
- *Used - Like New*: Dust cover is intact, with no nicks or tears. Spine has no signs of creasing. Pages are clean and not marred by notes or folds of any kind. It may contain remainder marks on outside edges, which should be noted in listing comments.
- *Used - Very Good*: Pages and dust cover are intact and not marred by notes or highlighting. The spine is undamaged.
- *Used - Good*: All pages and cover are intact (including the dust cover, if applicable). Spine may show signs of wear. Pages may include limited notes and highlighting. It may include "From the library of" labels.
- *Used - Acceptable*: All pages and the cover are intact, but the dust cover may be missing. Pages may include limited notes and highlighting, but the text cannot be obscured or unreadable.
- *Unacceptable*: This type has missing pages and obscured or unreadable text. We also do not permit the sale of advance reading copies, including uncorrected proofs, of in-print or not-yet-published books.

For a full explanation of Amazon's condition guidelines click on this link: http://www.amazon.com/gp/help/customer/display.html/ref=help_search_1-1?ie=UTF8andnodeId=200143590andqid=1425821202andsr=1-1

Summary of Book Listing with ScanLister

In a nut shell, here's how the Scanlister program works. You'll open up to a spreadsheet-like program. Select a default price and condition along with any notes that you would like to add in the comment section of the listing page (this is optional). Next, using your USB barcode scanner you scan through each book in order. Once you've scanned through each of your condition piles, then you change the condition of the books listed to the next group so, if you've finished listing all of your "Like New" books and you are moving onto "Very Good" books you would select "Very Good" from the drop-down menu. Once all of the scanning is finished, click on the button that will send all of this information off to Amazon.

Next, you'll need to log into Amazon, following the instructions from the ScanLister website, and find the batch of books that you just sent in. From the Manage FBA Shipment page, you'll find and select that particular shipment. From this page, you'll print out labels for your books in the order in which they were scanned, enter in how many boxes you'll be shipping and how much they weigh, accept the shipping charges and print out UPS shipping labels.

It might be a good idea for you to go through this process a few times so that you can write an accurate step-by-step instruction guide.

To download a free copy of the Listing and Shipping PDF Guide that we give to all of our Book-Lister go to:

http://profitsourcing.com/blog/listingandshipping.

Also, for a "high-level" view of our book listing process check out the Book-Listing Flow Chart which can be found at:
http://profitsourcing.com/blog/book-listing-flow-chart-using-scanlister

An alternate way to access both the Listing and Shipping guide, as well as the Book-Listing Flow Chart is to go to www.profitsourcing.com and click on the Book Flipping tab.

Other Listing Options

There are other options for listing books on Amazon. The two most popular web-based listing programs are ScanPower and Inventory Lab, and we've used them both. These programs are both very well designed, but I feel like they are a little too cumbersome for listing books at a rapid pace. If you'd like to check out these companies, they can be found at these links:

www.scanpower.com
www.inventorylab.com
www.ASellerTool.com

When it comes to listing the inventory that we buy through retail sourcing, we currently use Inventory Lab, which has some great accounting features.

In our "Members Only" area in the ProfitSourcing.com we've create training videos for Inventory Lab, ASellerTool's bulk upload program and ScanLister. If you're interesting in learning more about Book Flipping the Online Course go to:

Granting Permission to New Users on Your Amazon Selling Account

After the books have been scanned onto ScanLister, the person that you've hired to do your shipping will need to have access to your Amazon Seller Account. When I first considered having to do this, I was a little nervous. Even though we aim to hire people that we can trust, I really didn't want someone snooping around my entire online selling business, in areas that he/she had no need to be. The great thing about Amazon Seller Central is that you can set up unique logins for your users/employees and then chose what you would and wouldn't like them to have access to.

From the Seller Central homepage, click on the drop-down menu on the upper right-hand side of the page, and select User Permissions. Here you'll find a list of people and their email addresses that have access to your Amazon account. To set up a new user, simply send out an invitation by filling in the box at the top of the page. Don't worry, you'll have time to set up what this person will be able to access before they can open the account.

Once the invitation has been sent and accepted, then you can set up access restrictions. If you will be using ScanLister, you'll need to select these topics under the "View/edit" column, Item Classification Guide, Manage FBA Inventory/Shipments, Manage Inventory / Add a Product, Upload Inventory (all under the Inventory options), as well as Fulfillment Settings and Shipping Settings (both under the Settings options).

Setting Up a Free UPS Shipping Account

Now, all that's left to set up for your prepping and shipping system is a free UPS shipping account. This account will be used when you need to 1) order more UPS shipping labels and 2) when you need to schedule a UPS pickup.

UPS offers the most competitive shipping rates to Amazon 3rd party sellers. Since we are, in essence, partnering with Amazon, we can benefit from Amazon's partnered shipping rates with UPS. So we pay, what Amazon would pay, to ship something UPS ground. This is substantially cheaper and faster than any other shipping option, even the USPS. If you are shipping from an international location, not in the US, make sure you take a little time to ensure that you are selecting the best shipping option based on what's available to you.

If you plan on shipping a lot of packages via UPS you should take advantage of the free 2-up labels (two large blank stickers per sheet for box labels) that they offer to all of their UPS shipping accounts. Once your account has been set up on their website you can click on the "Shipping" tab and then select "Order Supplies". You are allowed to order 50 sheets at a time. If you need to order a case, just give UPS a call at 1-800-742-5877 and say that you would like to order item# 01774501 (which is a case of labels).

Setting up a UPS account is also necessary when the time comes to schedule UPS pickups. After the boxes have been packed, shipping labels printed and applied to the boxes, the next step is to get them out of your house or office and off to the Amazon fulfillment center. You can drop off UPS boxes for free at an authorized UPS drop off location, which includes all independently operated UPS Stores. But, if you decide you'd rather not lug around 50 pound boxes of books, you can schedule a UPS pick up instead.

If you had a day every week in which you would like UPS to come and pick up you could enroll in the UPS smart pickup program. If you're shipping sporadically and inconsistently, like ours is sometimes, you can always schedule pick-ups on demand. From the UPS homepage, click on the "Shipping" drop-down menu and select "Schedule a Pickup". Whether you schedule your pickups on demand or are enrolled in "Smart-Pickup" there is a small fee that is charged. You can set up automated billing online, or you can have invoices sent to your home or office.

If you are interested in having UPS come on certain days at certain times you may want to look into UPS Smart Pickup. In fact, last time I checked they were giving the first year away free.

For pickups on demand, the fees vary, I think that this has to do mainly with fuel costs since it seems to fluctuate up and down with gas prices, but for up to 30 boxes UPS will come pick them up for about $6-7.

Selling Professionally on Amazon

One other monthly fee to consider is $39.95 Professional Selling Account on Amazon. If you estimate that you will sell 40 items or more on Amazon per month, you'll want to sign up for a Pro Selling account. On every sale, Amazon will charge you a Per Transaction Fee of $1. If you are a Pro Seller, this fee is waived. So, of if you sell at least 40 items per month, then the membership will pay for itself, and could possibly save you some serious money if you sell more.

Calculating Start Up Costs

I figure now would be a good time to add up all of the expense thus far to get an estimate of how much a business, such as book-selling, would cost to get started.

Estimated Equipment and Supply Costs: $520.00

These estimated equipment and supply costs include a $200.00 scanning package, the $97.00 ScanLister program, 25 shipping boxes, 4 rolls of tape, 5 markers and 2 ink cartridges in addition to everything else on the suggested list above.

Estimated Monthly Fees: $70.00

These estimated fees include the $30.00 monthly, ASellerTool subscription and the $40 per month Amazon Professional Merchant account charge.

Total Estimated Start-up Costs: $590.00

That's not bad for start-up costs for a business that could bring in some excellent revenue! Obviously these figures don't include the cost of books sourced and commissions or finder's fees that you'll be paying your Book-Sourcers and Book-Listers. But, hopefully these estimates have given you a good idea of what it might cost to operate a business like this.

Regardless of whether you are planning on starting up a book-selling business or not, it is very important to consider the costs. Some business opportunities look really good on the surface but under the positivity, there could be hidden or overlooked costs that can stifle profitability.

Should Books Be Given Extra Protection?

There are some online sellers, who think that it is wise to give their books some added protection. So the question is, "Should we be bagging, shrink-wrapping or boxing our individual books before sending them off to Amazon?" Let me start off by saying that there isn't a "right" answer to this question. There are so many diverse ways that you can run your Amazon book selling business, so really the choice is yours.

Some online sellers insist on **poly-bagging** every book before they are shipped (a poly-bag is a think, clear plastic bag used to protect products).There are opportunities for your book to get a little dinged on the way to the fulfillment center, while it is in storage at the fulfillment center, and while it is in transit to the customer. A thick poly-bag would give the book some added protection.

Other book sellers insist on shrink-wrapping each book. A shrink-wrapped book would look much cleaner than one that is just poly bagged. Also, depending on how thick the plastic is, you could also add a little extra protection with this method.

Some sellers choose to box all of their books in individual cardboard book boxes. This would probably be the most expensive option of the three so far, but I imagine would offer the most protection.

Finally, other sellers are content sending their books in just as they are.

We do not bag, box, or wrap any of our books prior to labelling them and shipping them to Amazon. To prevent damage during transit to the Amazon Fulfilment Centers, we do our best to pack our 40-50lb boxes as tightly as possible. We figure that once the book arrives at the fulfilment center, it will be in good hands.

Amazon shelves their books on giant book shelves (library style) in their massive warehouses, and we have rarely had any problems with the customer receiving a damaged book. To avoid negative customer experiences, we will sometimes downgrade the condition of the book to account for a smudge here or a ding there in transit. Even though the lower condition means that we have to charge lower prices, we figure that we make up for it in the saved time and shipping expenses.

Figure 50

As you can see from this picture of an Amazon Fulfilment Center (Figure 50), all of their books are stored on giant book shelves. From my perspective, most of these books are "naked", meaning they aren't poly-bagged, shrink-wrapped, or boxed.

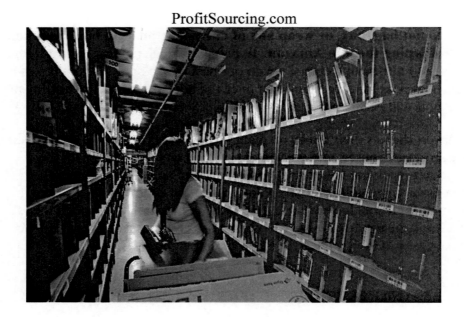

Amazon has quite the efficient system for receiving, storing, and distributing books to their customers once the order is placed. So, for the sake of efficiency and to avoid the added expense of boxes, bags, or wrap, we feel comfortable sending our books in "as is."

Ultimately, we want the customer to be happy with the book that they receive from us. **If you feel uneasy about how your book will be handled before and after it arrives at the warehouse, you should take some protective measures.** Or, if you choose to just box, bag, or wrap the more expensive books, you could do that too.

Just make sure that you consider the added expenses of using one of these methods and spend some time thinking about their overall effect on your COGS (Cost of Goods Sold).

What is a "Collectable" Book?

Only approved sellers can sell "collectable" books. Here is the definition of a collectable book according to Amazon's Terms & Conditions:

To ensure that customers are able to buy with confidence from all sellers on Amazon.com, sellers listing in the Collectable Books category must be pre-approved.

To be considered collectable, a book must be unique in a way that could reasonably be assumed to increase the book's value to a collector:

- First editions and first printings
- Signed, inscribed, or scarce copies
- Advance reading copies and uncorrected proofs of out-of-print books

Note: The sale of uncorrected proofs of in-print or not-yet-published books is prohibited.

Collectible books do not include the following:

- Former library books
- Remaindered books
- Book club editions

Conventional wisdom says that "collectable" books, books that have unique, one-of-a-kind value would be better sold on eBay. While this may still be the case, if you have a continuous source of books of this nature, it may be worth your time to check in with Amazon from time-to-time. As the Amazon customer evolves over time, maybe a demand for these unique books will grow.

Another option would be to have your books listed on both Amazon and eBay simultaneously. That way, you could have your books in front of both eBay and Amazon buyers. This added exposure could be huge for your bottom line. How could one accomplish this? Is there an easy way to have a product on both marketplaces simultaneously? Let's just say, you have options.

You could MF the book on Amazon and also have the book listed on eBay. If the book sells on one marketplace, you would have to manually go onto the other to cancel the listing or delete the inventory. These hard-to-find books probably won't sell at the exact same time, so as long as you check in once every day or so you should be fine. The worst case scenario would be if you sold the same book on both platforms and had to refund one of the customers for not having enough copies on hand.

The downside to this is that you won't be able to sell your book on Amazon via FBA. As we have already discussed, selling FBA is good for business (sales velocity and profitability), so it would be sort of a bummer to not be able to take advantage of that. There is another option though…

Multi-Channel Fulfilment

Amazon is happy if you use their fulfilment centers to multi-channel fulfil your inventory. What does multi-channel fulfilment mean, exactly? This is how it works: you have your items (that are currently being stored at a fulfilment center) listed for sale available on multiple market places. For instance, let's say that you're selling a vintage board game. You have this game listed in Collectable - Very Good on Amazon, and at the same time, to take advantage of the "vintage" hunters on eBay, you have it listed on that site as well. If a customer orders your product on eBay, you would go into your Amazon account, you'd locate the game on your Manage Inventory page, and you would elect to have it removed.

On the Amazon seller central page, you would be instructed to enter the address and recipient of the package, and you'd be given some options as to how you'd like the package shipped. You should have it over-nighted, sent in 2 days, or a few other slower options. You'd select the option that matches what you advertised on the eBay listing, agree to pay some reasonable fees, and have the item shipped off to the customer.

The benefit here is that you have this particular item listed for sale on multiple platforms, and at the same time, can take advantage of Amazon world-class distribution. It's important to count the cost. There are some fees involved with the fulfilment of these orders, but for many of the items that you'd like to sell on eBay, this partnership may be a good fit.

Plus, it doesn't end with eBay. You can virtually sell your items on any other website and then at the click of a few buttons, you can have one of them shipped to a customer. You don't need to have any on hand, which means that you can run this multi-site business from anywhere in the world (as long as you have access to the internet). Truly, the possibilities are endless.

Think about it, your books could be listed on:
Amazon.com
eBay.com
Alibris.com
AbeBooks.com

There are some technology companies that will help automate this whole process. They will allow you to list your items on a variety of marketplaces, and you won't have to worry about multiple sales coming through for the same item and/or having to cancel the book on a handful of other marketplaces once it sells. Check out:

SellerEngine.com
AutoMCF.com
StitchLabs.com

Multi-Channel Fulfilment Fees

Before you should even consider adding MCF to your portfolio, it may be important to count the costs. Just remember that you will now be able to offer your customers, across all platforms, the same logistical benefits that are currently only available to Prime Members and those who achieve Super Saver Shipping status, namely guaranteed 2-day shipping or overnight shipping service.

If you'd like to check out the full gamut of MCF options and terms go to this URL:
http://www.amazon.com/gp/help/customer/display.html/?nodeId=2002404
60

Here's the MCF fees for Standard-Sized Media (Figure 51):

Standard-Size Media

Fees for Multi-Channel Fulfillment orders placed off Amazon.com apply to domestic orders. See FBA Export for international pricing.

Fulfillment Fee		Shipping Method		
		Standard	Expedited (two-day)	Priority (Next Day)
Order Handling per order		$1.90	$7.40	$14.40
Pick & Pack per Unit		$0.60	$0.60	$0.60
Weight Handling* per lb.	First 15 lb.	$0.45	$0.55	$1.50
	+ next 16-70 lb.	$0.45	$0.70	$1.75
	+ next 71-150 lb.	$0.45	$0.85	$2.00

Figure 51

Okay, so let's take this chart and break these fees down.

Standard-Size Media

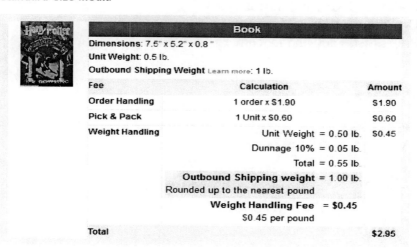

Book		
Dimensions: 7.5" x 5.2" x 0.8 "		
Unit Weight: 0.5 lb.		
Outbound Shipping Weight Learn more: 1 lb.		
Fee	Calculation	Amount
Order Handling	1 order x $1.90	$1.90
Pick & Pack	1 Unit x $0.60	$0.60
Weight Handling	Unit Weight = 0.50 lb.	$0.45
	Dunnage 10% = 0.05 lb.	
	Total = 0.55 lb.	
	Outbound Shipping weight = 1.00 lb.	
	Rounded up to the nearest pound	
	Weight Handling Fee = $0.45	
	$0.45 per pound	
Total		$2.95

So, a pretty typical sized book would cost $2.95 for Amazon to fulfil ($1.90 + $0.60 + $0.45 = $2.95), which really isn't that bad at all, especially considering that Amazon will handle all of the work (packing, labelling and shipping). $2.95 will get standard shipping. If you wanted it expedited (two-day), it would cost you an extra $.10 and priority (Next Day) and extra $1.30.

Conclusion

My recommendation is to go through the entire shipping process yourself and document all of the steps along the way. This way when or if you decide to outsource the shipping aspect of your online selling business, you'll be able to efficiently and accurately train someone else to do the job properly and with clarity.

Step #1 Acquire a Barcode Scanner
Step #2 Outsource With FBA
Step #3 Establish Book-buying Criteria
Step #4 Locate and Research Local Thrift-stores
Step #5 Do Some Scanning Yourself
Step #6 Prep., List, Pack and Document

Step #7: Establish How Your People Will Pay and be Paid

"If you value your team, they will know it in a lot of ways, and one of the ways is that they'll be paid and paid well."
Dave Ramsey, from his book *EntreLeadership*.

Show Me the Money!

If you haven't noticed yet, I'm all about keeping it simple, and when it comes to paying my people I don't deviate from that norm. There are many sellers out there that have complex compensation plans that take into account a finder's fee and some sort of after-the-sale commission.

We pay our people up front. We found that most people crave a regular, dependable source of income. I would really freak some people out, especially if they were working for me full time, if I suggested that they would only make a commission after the item had sold. Would that really be fair? Well, it may be fair, but would my workers appreciate it? Wouldn't it be better to help them find good quality items at a discount and then just pay them a flat rate up front? I think so. I would appeal to you that most people, who are looking for a part-time job, would be happy taking a little less, if they were guaranteed some money for their efforts. So, should we pay our people hourly or according to some other metric? The way I look at it is if you're not going to pay them on commission then the other options would be to pay hourly, pay a percentage of the purchase price or pay a flat amount per item.

Paying hourly

As soon as you start paying your employee's hourly you have subliminally created within them criteria for success that I feel could run in complete contradiction to your company goals. You've clearly defined success for your workers. You've said to them, "If you would like to be successful and make lots of money, be sure to put in lots of hours." A successful day for them will very easily be determined based on how many hours they have put in, whereas the amount of hours worked doesn't necessarily mean that they have had a productive day, right? We don't want our workers to have the desire to maximize the amount of hours that they've put in, we want them to produce.

If my Book-Sourcer goes out and strikes up a deal with a local recycling center and he is given 500 textbooks that were discarded, still in great condition, by the local public school, and it only takes him an hour - well, take the rest of the day off my friend! Go spend time at home with your family!

There has to be another way to pay our employee's that demonstrates to them that we want them to produce and that we value their time too much to hold them to an hourly schedule. I know that some jobs require an hourly pay, but not when it comes to outsourcing your Amazon business, or any business that is similar. Can you see what I'm saying? I want to have a team that is not fueled by the desire to trade dollars for hours. I want them to be fueled to achieve goals, exceed expectations, form partnerships and find success. If that only takes them 20 hours a week then that's great! So, if we don't pay them hourly, how do we pay them?

Paying on Percentage

There are a few ways, other than hourly pay, to compensate your shoppers. You could instead pay them a percentage of the buy cost. What is the "buy cost" you say? Well, if they spend $200 at a library sale on books you could pay them a percentage of what they spent to buy books (that met your criteria, of course). We don't compensate our Book-Sourcers or Book-Listers this way, but I'll give you an example. Our retail arbitrage shoppers (non-book product finders) are paid 10% of the buy-cost on all retail purchases that meet our guidelines. If they spend $1000 at Target they would have earned $100, and if it only took them 2 hours then they just made $50/hour. On the other hand, if it takes them 3 hours to spend $300 then they will only make $10/hour.

Now, there is a concern that with this model of compensation, your worker may legitimately be working hard but unable to find much of anything. How discouraging would that be? To work an 8 hour day with nothing to show for it! If you take the steps above and provide a good foundation for success this shouldn't be an issue. Making their sourcing trip as efficient as possible and leaving the guesswork out of their job will help them be successful. We want our people to exceed their own expectations and we work really hard to make that happen. Secretly, we would never let them flounder or struggle for long. If one of our retail shoppers put in long hours and had nothing to show for it, we would offer them some sort of hourly compensation until they got back on their feet. We've never had to do this before, but we would.

Do you think that paying a retail shopper over $30/hour on average is too much? We don't, and here's why. We want to attract and keep the best talent, and one way to do that is to pay good money for hard work done (more on hiring Top Talent in the next step). But, I should get back to books...

Paying a Flat Finder's Fee

The compensation plan that we have set up for our Book-Sourcers is pretty simple. We pay them $1 per book sourced, as long as it meets our buying criteria. So, if they go to a local thrift store and spend an hour finding 25 books, they have just made $25. They don't have to wait until the books sell, they get paid every week. Just like paying on a percentage, paying them a dollar per book encourages them to find the most amount of books in the least amount of time. If they go to a book sale and hustle through the non-fiction section and come out with over 100 books in an hour, they are really happy, and you know what we are really happy too!

The great thing about this compensation plan is that the finder's fee has already be taken into account when setting the criteria and since the ROI for books is so big, even after paying our Book-Sourcers, there still is plenty of room for profit.

How We Pay Our Book People

We have three different, sometimes interchangeable types of positions in our book-selling company. There are people who go out and source books for us, people who prep, label and ship books to Amazon and we also have a manager who oversees the entire operation. Each position is compensated differently.

Book-Sourcing: $1/book
Book-Listing: $.25/book
Book-Sourcing and Listing Manager: $.25/book

We already covered book sourcing, so I will spend some time highlighting the other two types of positions within our company.

The Book-Lister

Currently we have two part-time Book Listers and one full-time Book Lister and they do a fantastic job! After books have been purchased by our Book Sourcers they are dropped off at the house of our Book Lister. He then preps the books, so that they are in presentable and sell-able condition. This includes removing price-tags or labels and quickly cleaning the cover. This is also a good time to go flip through the book to determine its listing condition (Acceptable, Good, Very Good, Like New or New) while at the same time unfolding any dog-eared corners and removing any marks in the book. Basically, we need to make the book look as presentable as possible.

We encourage our Book Lister not to spend too much time on each book. Once again, we want them to succeed and success to them means a maximum amount of books listed. For the time spent listing books for us, he or she is paid $.25/book. Just like our Book Sourcers, we strive to put our Book Lister in a position to succeed. We provide them with all of the tools and training to ensure that they will hit the ground running. The book listing system is a pretty simple system to learn so we have found that the people that we have hired have picked up on it pretty quick.

One of the perks of being the Book Lister is that you get to work from home. We have it set up so that the Book Sourcers drop off books at the Book Lister's house, and once the shipment has been packed the Lister can schedule a UPS pickup, which means they never have to leave the house!

If you're interested in what $.25/book would equate to in an hourly wage, I would estimate that our guy makes about $15-20/hour.

Book Sales Manager

Managing this entire operation, from a logistical standpoint, would have proven to be too challenging. We live nearly two hours away from the major metropolitan area in which we conduct the majority of our book sourcing. With all of the other responsibilities that I have at home and with other areas of the online selling business that garner my attention, there was no way that I would have been able to oversee all aspects of this books selling business adequately. Not to mention, we wanted this business to be fully outsourced, and we found the perfect guy to be our manager.

Andrew, who happens to be my brother-in-law, is a naturally gifted leader and business man. When I ran the book sales management position by him, he jumped at the opportunity. It is very important to hire top talent if you'd like to have consistency and growth in your businesses, especially for a managerial type position, and for us, this was the guy (more on hiring top talent in Step #8). The way that we have this partnership arranged is that Andrew works with us as an independent contractor. He owns his own Book Sourcing and Listing Management Company and we pay him to oversee our operation.

We pay for all of the supplies, software, inventory and equipment, but all other business expenses are Andrew's responsibly. We felt that this arrangement was the most favorable arrangement for all parties involved. If you are interested in exploring the options of how to structure your company, I would encourage you to do some research. There are other options out there than the traditional approach. Be sure to run your decision, whatever it is, by a paid profession just to ensure you comply with any state or federal laws.

As our Book Sales Manager, Andrew's responsibilities are to:
1. Hire and Train in new Book-Listers and Book-Sourcers
2. Coordinate sourcing in an organized fashion to avoid any overlap
3. Manage and encourage current Listers and Sourcers
4. Be vision-minded and on the lookout for opportunities to expand
5. Offer technical support as it's needed
6. Be in regular contact with ownership in regards to the health and future of the business

When choosing someone to manage a significant aspect of your business, make sure that you choose very carefully. Hire or partner with someone who is outgoing, a gifted leader, and someone who can catch your vision for the company and get really excited about it. To be successful as a manager in this business, you will need to find ways to self-motivate. No longer will there be a boss, looking over your shoulder, telling you when to start working, when to have lunch and when to go home. The hardest part of this online selling business, for some, is just getting out of bed in the morning. Make sure that you hire someone with drive and initiative, someone who has ambitions that match yours and a reason to get out of bed in the morning to look for ways to be productive and to grow the business.

Coming up with a compelling job description

The goal is to help attract the right job candidates. Knowing what kind of person that you're looking for is the first step, but the next step is to get the word out to those who might be interested. Whether you have a family member, a friend, or perfect strangers in mind, having a good job description for the position will help everyone understand the perks and expectations of the job.

According to sba.gov (The U.S. Small Business Administration), an effective job description will:
- Help Attract the right job candidates
- Describe the major areas of an employee's job or position
- Serve as a major basis for outlining performance expectations, job training, job evaluation, and career advancement
- Provide a reference point for compensation decisions and un-fair hiring practices

A job description should be practical, clear, and accurate to effectively define your needs. Good job descriptions typically begin with a careful analysis of the important facts about a job such as:
- Individual tasks involved
- The methods used to complete the tasks
- The purpose and responsibilities of the job
- The relationship of the job to other jobs
- Qualifications needed for the job

Following those guidelines, I'll share what I've come up with in regard to Job descriptions for the positions that we're looking to fill.

Book Sourcer Job Description:

Title: Book Sourcing Specialist
"Locating, evaluating, and buying books that meet the company's buying criteria"

Summary: Book Sourcing Specialists play an exciting role in our online book selling business. Their primary task is to, with the help of technology, locate and buy books that can potentially be sold for a profit online.

Book Sourcing Specialists will spend their time at places were books are being sold. This will include but not be limited to: library sales, thrift stores, garage sales, book stores, and other book-selling events.

List of tasks that are necessary for success:
- Desire and ability to learn new technology
- Willingness to scan books (using a laser scanner on the book's barcode) at crowded book sales and thrift stores
- An outgoing nature that would welcome negotiations with store/sales management
- The physical ability to lift, push, and pull dozens of pounds of books around a sale or store
- Organizational skills necessary for basic bookkeeping
- Professional conduct and communication with company management and those working the sales and thrift stores where sourcing will occur
- A desire to learn new things, a teachable approach to this business
- The ability to make adaptations to sourcing strategy should the market indicate that a change is necessary.

- A thrill of the hunt. Sourcing books is like looking for treasure; the motivation to find more books will be crucial to helping a Book Sourcer really succeed in this business

Our goal is to help all of our Book Sourcers succeed; therefore we will do all that we can to put them into a position to maximize the number of books they will be able to find.

Compensation:
$1/book sourced that meets the criteria

To what does this translate per hour?
We have chosen a compensation package that we feel is best for both parties involved. We will put you in a position to be able to reasonably source between 20-40 books per hour. Although we cannot make any guarantees, we will be sure that we do all that we can to help you maximize your book sourcing trips.

Equipment that will be supplied:
PDA (Portable Digital Assistant) loaded with the Amazon database
Laser scanner (for quickly scanning barcodes)
All of the cords and other accessories necessary to use equipment

What you'll need to bring to the table:
- Reliable transportation to and from sourcing locations and to deliver books to their next stop (a local Book Lister).

- Access to a computer (PC), with an internet connection, so that you can update the PDA on a weekly basis. The ASellerTool program is downloaded onto the computer and the PDA is connected through a USB port.

- An email address, so that buying reports can be sent in every other week so that you can be compensated for the books you've purchased. A scanner or camera for taking pictures of all receipts.

- A way to pay for the books at the point of sale. We recommend that you open a credit card account and then we'll reimburse you when we pay you for your bi-weekly commissions. Other options can be discussed if this proves problematic.

If you have any questions or concerns about the job and/or would like to set up an interview, please get in contact Andrew (the Books Sales Manager) @ (xxx) xxx-xxxx or Andrew@xxxxx.com

Feel free to use this job description, or a variation of it, to attract local talent. Even if you plan on hiring someone that you already know, having a clean list of expectations could prove to be very helpful down the road.

Here's the job description for our Book Listing Position:

Book Sourcer Job Description:

Title: Book Listing Specialist
"Sorting, Preparing, Listing and Shipping Books, in bulk, off to Amazon to be Sold."

Summary: Book Listing Specialists have the benefit of making good money while working at home. You'll acquire books that have been purchased by our Book Sourcers, and you'll be in charge of preparing them to be sold. This process involves removing price tags, assessing the books' condition (according to Amazon's Terms and Conditions), listing the books (using the programs and tools provided), and finally, boxing and shipping them off.

List of tasks that are necessary for success:
- Desire and ability to learn new technology
- Willingness to master the art of label scraping
- Good attention to detail so that books are assessed correctly, and the right books are sent to the right places
- The physical ability to lift, push, and pull dozens of pounds of books.
- Organizational skills necessary for basic bookkeeping

- Professional conduct and communication with company management and our Book Sourcers
- A desire to learn new things, a teachable approach to this business
- The ability to make adaptations to sourcing strategy should the market indicate that a change is necessary.

Compensation:
$0.25/book prepped & listed

To what does this translate per hour?
We have chosen a compensation package that we feel is best for both parties involved. We will put you in a position to be able to reasonably prepare and list between 50-100 books per hour.

Equipment & Supplies that we will provide:
- Scotty Peelers for Scrapping Labels
- Heat Gun
- Rubbing Alcohol
- Paper Towels
- Printer Ink
- USB laser barcode scanner
- Sheets of Blank Address Labels
- Small and Medium-Sized Boxes for Books
- Downloadable Listing Software

What you'll need to bring to the table:
- A safe place to store and list the books before they are shipped
- A personal computer (PC), which will be used to list the books and prepare the outgoing shipments
- A standard-sized printer
- The ability to make small purchases for supplies for which you'll be reimbursed bi-weekly

If you have any questions or concerns about the job and/or would like to set up an interview, please get in contact Andrew (the Books Sales Manager) @ (xxx) xxx-xxxx or Andrew@xxxxx.com

After hiring some Book Sourcers and Book Listers, you may decide that you'd like to also bring in a Book Sales Manager. We started our Book Sales Manager as a Book Sourcer, so he could get some on-the-job experience, as well as, have a first-hand point of view of the geography. But, during the interview with him, the expectation, out of the gate, was that he would someday soon manage the whole operation, so we could focus our energies elsewhere.

Here's the Book Sales Manager's job description:

Book Sales Manager Job Description:

Title: Book Sales Manager

"Overseeing the whole book selling business; hiring, training, encouraging, taking corrective action, and firing Book Sourcers and Book Listers (if necessary).

Working hand-in-hand with business owners to ensure that the bookselling business is hitting all of its financial goals. Clearly communicating expectations with the team and working hard to ensure a high morale. Thinking outside the box to find the best sources of inventory at the lowest price."

Summary: Book Sales Managers have the opportunity to put their managerial strengths into action. This position is ideally suited for people that have solid leadership qualities. Book Sourcers and Listers will be dependent on you for their success.

List of tasks that are necessary for success:
- Desire and ability to learn new technology
- Willingness to master the art of online book selling
- Good attention to detail so that Book Sourcers and Book Listers are properly trained

- A good understanding of how the business works so that you can adequately train others
- Organizational skills necessary for basic bookkeeping
- Professional conduct and communication with company management and our Book Sourcers & Listers
- A desire to learn new things, a teachable approach to this business
- The ability to make adaptations to managerial strategy should the market indicate that a change is necessary.

Compensation:
$0.25/book sourced by your Book Sourcers
$0.10/book listed by your Book Listers

To what does this translate per hour?
Obviously, as your network of Book Sourcers and Listers grows, you can expect better compensation. Much of the work that you put in, up front, will contribute to solid earnings down the road. Here's an example of reasonable goals for the first couple of months:

In 2 months you could have two Book Sourcers who are sourcing 1000 books/week and one Book Lister preparing and shipping all of those books to Amazon.

Estimated weekly earnings based on those 2 month numbers: $250 (Book Sourcing Commission) + $100 (Book Listing Commission) = $350/week.

Obviously, these conservative numbers don't add up to much of a weekly income, but it is something that can be built upon.

What you'll need to bring to the table:
- A personal computer (PC), which will be used to regularly communicate with business owners and Book Sourcers and Book Listers

- The ability to make small purchases for supplies for which you'll be reimbursed bi-weekly

If you have any questions or concerns about the job and/or would like to set up an interview, please get in contact Andrew (the Books Sales Manager) @ (xxx) xxx-xxxx or Andrew@xxxxx.com

I understand that these numbers for the Book Sales Manager probably don't wow and amaze, but there's tons of potential. Our Book Sales Manager only works about 3 days a week, and he is pulling in some great commissions. It has taken him about a year to put in place a very solid network of Sourcers and Listers. The key is finding someone who is willing to work hard and will be able to catch on to your entrepreneurial vision for the company. If he/she is also doing some Book Sourcing, this could help a financial situation as things are falling into place.

If you'd prefer to play a more active managerial role in your business, you could cut out the Book Sales Manager position all together. That's the beauty of this business. You can structure it any way that you choose. If you have good training and an encouragement system, it really might not be that much extra work. For us, having a Book Sales Manager in place really allows us to free our time and energy so that we can focus on other business endeavours.

How to Measure Performance

Each Book Sourcer is linked to the particular books that they have sourced. This is accomplished by having the Book-Lister assign a special MSKU number to each different Book Sourcer. MSKU is an acronym that stands for Merchant Stock Keeping Unit, and it is a way for Amazon sellers to keep track of their inventory. You can choose whatever letter and number combination that you'd like. The MSKU is not visible by the customer and is only for the sellers benefit. For example, if a particular shipment of books was sourced by David, the Book-Lister would put his name into ScanLister followed by a number that progressively and automatically gets larger. This way we can sort our book inventory by Book Sourcer. Also, when books sell we can quickly to determine who's book it was.

We keep any eye on all of the inventory that our Book Sourcers buy. If we were to see an excessive amount of books that are obviously not meeting the criteria, then we would be communicate with our Book-Sales Manager to address the problem and offer additional training. Also, we keep an eye on customer feedback as a measure for the quality of work that is being done by our Book-Lister. If we are flooded with positive comments, from our Amazon customers, about the accuracy and condition of the book they received, we feel like this reflects nicely on the work of our Lister. He/she is obviously conditioning the books properly and preparing them in a way that pleases our customers.

Occasionally, we will receive some negative feedback for a book that we sold that has proven unsatisfactory to our customers. We are quick to offer dissatisfied customers a refund, and we will note the issue so that it can be forwarded to the applicable Book-Lister and/or Book-Sourcer.

The greatest measure of worker performance is the number of books sourced or the number of books listed. We are always looking for ways to make our company a great company to work for. Recognizing hard work can often times trump financial compensation. Be on the lookout for and acknowledge hard work. It is always better to make an error that leans toward too much praise and recognition, than to give far too little. Appreciating your Book-Sourcers and Book-Listers can be done in a number of ways an here are a few examples: make a post on your Facebook page expressing your satisfaction for exceptional work, send an email, send a handwritten letter, and buy gifts for your workers throughout the year.

Book Sourcing/Listing Budget

Near the end of Q1 2015, we ran into some major cash flow problems. Due to a variety of factors, which I will discuss in a moment, we were basically spending WAY more money than we were bringing in. This meant that some changes needed to be made in a hurry, unless we wanted to run the risk of having to shut things down for a bit. The problem was that turning off the business was really not an option since we had 2 independent contractors that are very dependent on the money that they make sourcing and listing books for us. We had to find solutions, and we had to find them fast.

Here's the breakdown. We were spending more than $5,000 per week to run the business. This included book costs, equipment, supplies, and Book Sourcers, Listers, and Managerial commissions. The problem was that we were in the middle of March, and we were only bringing in $3,000 in profit on average per week.

I could have gotten really discouraged. My wife, the more analytical one, began to really worry about the future of our bookselling business, since this lack of profit began to intrude on other areas of business and life.

After exhausting a very large list of possible contributing factors, we narrowed the reasons down to 3 things. Due to a combination of these three things, we found ourselves in a tough situation.

1. Our books were not getting listed and sent in fast enough.
The net result of this inefficiency was that we had several thousand books sitting at our Book Managers place waiting to get listed and shipped. We had recently lost a couple Book Listers and found ourselves, all of a sudden, without the personnel to keep up. We made getting those books listed a top priority. Our goal for this business is to ensure that we can sell as many or more per week than we are taking in, and one huge reason this wasn't happening was that thousands of dollars worth of profitable inventory was stuck in limbo. As soon as all of these books hit the warehouse, sales began to pick up in a big way.

2. We tried to expand too fast.
In the span of about 2 months, we hired a new Book Sourcer / Book Lister and sent him to Milwaukee. We hired a cross-country trucker to source books when his company required him to take mandatory breaks along his route. The problem lies in the area of expectations. My Book Sales Manager, who does all of the hiring, training, and firing, sent our Milwaukee guy out to source and list books as his sole source of income. I, on the other hand, assumed that he had a full-time job and was planning to source and list books a few days per week. So, when he started sourcing upwards of 600 books per week, it put immediate and unexpected strain on our business. At the very same time, this trucker guy that we hired was

sort of a question mark. We weren't sure if this souring thing would work for him. Not only did it work out, he crushed it out there. If we would have let him go completely, he probably could have sourced more than our Milwaukee guy. He was getting some good quality books, at excellent acquisitions costs (less than $1/book), but we were sort of blindsided by all of this sourcing success.

3. We were in the slow time of the year for book sales.
March through July have, historically, been slow months for book sales nationally. Once August comes around, the book selling market picks up in a big way, and sales continue to impress until the end of February.

So, it was really the combination of these three things that put a lot of pressure on our business. Honestly, I think if one of these three contributing factors hadn't been an issue, we would have done just fine. Such as, if #1 & 2 happened in the month of September, for example, we would not have really noticed the financial strain, because all of our other inventory would have been selling at an accelerated rate and price, and we would have been able to cover these unexpected inventory and expansion issues. Or, if our books had been consistently and efficiently listed and shipped, we would have had the revenue to cover a downtime in sales and our quick expansion into other regions. You get the idea.

When these problems landed on our doorstep, a part of me embraced them as an opportunity to grow our business. I know if we were able to successfully get through this adversity, we would have a better run company in the end as a result. The hard work that we put into isolating the problem and then coming up with procedural solutions would mean that we would be a better organization in the end.

Here's what we did to solve the immediate problem and put in safeguards that would protect our business from similar problems in the future.

1. We got serious about ensuring that books are listed and shipped in a timely matter.
Thousands of books sitting around, waiting to get listed is not an option. Being in-between Book Listers is not an excuse. If it means that the Book Sales Manager has to stop and do some book listing before he/she gets to

do some more sourcing, so be it. Our Book Sales Manager is great; he really works hard at doing everything possible to ensure that we are running a profitable business. We are, from here on out, going to be more mindful about how many books are coming and how many books are going out. If we see a trend, over the course of a couple of weeks, of more books coming in than being listed and shipped, then it will be investigated. As soon as those books hit the warehouse, the cash flow problem quickly started to go away.

2. To solve the unexpected expansion issue, we put a Sourcing, Listing, & Managerial budget into place.
Actually, this budget solved a lot of our problems. I'll get into the specifics of it here shortly, but it suffices to say, we would give our Book Sales Manager a budget from which he needed to allocate to all areas of the business. Because this budget was closely tied to the previous period's profitability, the more money we were able to bring, in the more the budget would be. This subliminally would encourage a higher quality of books sourced, a reason to get books listed and shipped as quickly as possible, as well as, a more focused plan for expansion and growth.

3. Finally, we need to be mindful of where we are in the calendar year.
I don't think that this issue, isolated on its own, would be an issue without some of the other contributing factors. But, it is a good idea to know where our business is in the cycle of things, so we can plan accordingly. We're okay to spend more money than we make in Q2 and part of Q3, because we know that our big payout is coming starting in August. However, we can never afford a $2,000 net loss per week.

All in all, don't be afraid when obstacles present themselves. In fact, expect them and embrace them when they do. Hopefully, one of the things that you can learn from what we went through in Q2 of 2015 is that a true entrepreneur problem with our business intrinsically provided a vehicle to help our business grow. The net result of this challenge, that our book business faced, helped us come out the other end as a stronger and more efficiently run company, which is great!

Step #1 Acquire a Barcode Scanner
Step #2 Outsource With FBA
Step #3 Establish Book-buying Criteria
Step #4 Locate and Research Local Thrift-stores
Step #5 Do Some Scanning Yourself
Step #6 Prep., List, Pack and Document
Step #7 Establish How Your People Will Pay and Be Paid

Step #8 Hire Top Talent

"If you pick the right people and give them the opportunity to spread their wings and put compensation as a carrier behind it, you almost don't have to manage them."
Jack Welch, former CEO of GE.

"I hire people brighter than me and I get out of the way."
Lee Iacocca

Building Your Team the Right Way

I know the temptation's there to hire mediocre workers and pay them mediocre money. There are many online sellers who pay their employee's a very low hourly wage, but then are frustrated when they aren't producing quite up to par with their expectations or when they quit to find a new job. Don't do it! Life happens, we live in an imperfect world, so there will always be some unpredictability in business when working with people, but I recommend that you do everything in your power to hire and keep employees who are motivated to produce at a high level. But what kind of people should we hire? What should we look for in a perspective employee? What character traits? Should there be advancement opportunities in place? How do employees or workers get raises? These are all great questions, let's get the answers!

Determine Your Strengths and Weaknesses

The first step in building a great team is to determine what your own personal strengths and weaknesses are. This can be done a variety of ways. There are a number of books and tests that you can take that will reveal your strengths and weaknesses, such as the Myers-Briggs personality test or the StrengthFinders assessment. Both of these tests may prove helpful in helping you determine your entrepreneurial make up. Another way to determine what makes you strong as a business leader may be to just sit down with a pen and paper to conduct a self evaluation. What do you do exceptionally well? Are you really analytical and good with numbers or are you more of an abstract-minded visionary? Are you a very thoughtful introvert or do you excel most around people? Are you a salesman? Can you wheel and deal with the best of them? Or, do you prefer to find other strategic ways to get a deal? Ask yourself these questions and more, really try to dig deep. It also may be a good idea to get some feedback on your strengths and weakness from someone close to you, someone who knows you and wouldn't mind being brutally honest with you about areas that you are strong and weak in.

Once you've figured out your strengths, now conversely, determine the areas in which you are weak. Building a successful team means filling in the gaps. You'll want to find people who are strong in the areas that you're weak, so that as a complimentary group you'll be an organization to be reckoned with.

The temptation is to determine what areas that you're weak in and then to devote a significant amount of time to trying to get better in those areas, but I think that this strategy is a waste of time. It would be better for you to recognize the areas that God has gifted you in and invest and highlight those areas while finding others to fill in the gaps. This philosophical approach to business is applied by many of the successful entrepreneurs today.

General Traits to Look for in an Employee

When trying to determine whether or not to welcome someone on the team, what should you be looking for? Should we hire any family member or friend that is out of work? Would it be better to have some sort of criteria to reference? What traits do top CEOs look for in star employees? According to an article in INC magazine these are Top 7 Traits of Star Employees: http://www.inc.com/drew-hendricks/top-7-traits-of-star-employees.html

1. **Happiness** – No one wants to work with grumpy people. Happiness also reflects the ability to tackle challenges without being discouraged.
2. **Creativity** – Innovative people are an asset at every level within an organization.
3. **Hustle** – People need to have a solid hard-working, mindset if they are going to be one of your best employees.
4. **Flexibility** – Someone who is willing to do whatever it takes, within reason, to help the company succeed.
5. **Honesty** – Trust is one of the most important characteristics to look for in a perspective employee. Dedicated, honest work is necessary for lasting success in business.
6. **Passion** – Find people who will be really excited and motivated by their role in the company. Their "why" will need to be greater than money if they really want to excel.

7. **Confidence** – Top CEOs want to see confidence in the ability to succeed in their perspective employees.

This is a great list. Due to the nature of the online selling industry, I would like to add one more trait. When looking to hire someone for a position in our company, we look for someone who is self-motivated. Most of the time, our employees and contractors choose their own working hours. They can shop where and when they feel like it, for the most part. This type of set up offers the people who work for us an excellent amount of freedom and flexibility, but this freedom and flexibility has its own set of temptations. Since no one tells them where to be and when to be there, they need to be able to get themselves out of bed and off to work on their own. This is why we look for people who have drive and ambition. This way the shift to a more freeing work schedule won't be an issue.

You Get What You Pay For

Your ability to attract top talent in your company rests mostly on your ability to compensate them in accordance with their expectations. What I like about our flat-fee compensation plan is that it really gives our workers an excellent opportunity to make some nice money. Coupled with the other perks of working in a position such as those mentioned above like work schedule flexibility, the benefit of working from home (book-listing), the freedom to travel and shop (book-sourcing), and the promise of being able to lead people and manage a business (book-manager). Good hard working, qualified people are encouraged to come and stay.

Finding Good, Hardworking People

If you're willing to pay above market value for your people, then you can expect to be able to find above average talent. In fact, with the compensation set up the way that we have it, there are tons of growth opportunities for those who really get out there and hustle. One of our "full-time" Book Sourcers (book sourcing is his sole source of income) chooses to only work three days a week so that he can spend the rest of his week working on other things that he's passionate about. The money's good and there is tons of freedom and flexibility.

As I mentioned above, you will have positions available that will promise to pay some good money ($15-20+/hour working from home as a Book Lister, and $30+/hour working as a Book Sourcer). Both of these positions come with tons of flexibility and growth opportunity.

The great thing about this business is that people you know, who would like to make some extra money, can do so first on a part-time basis, which will act as a trial run for both you and them. If after the first few weeks, they hate it, they can move on. Likewise, if you find their work-ethic to be less than desirable, you can also make the decision to find talent elsewhere. That being said, if you are careful about whom you hire, and you make sure that you are hiring people, who have all the intangibles that could position themselves for success in this business, you should be able to find a good match. But, where should you look to fill these positions?

Hiring people to work for your company can be such a daunting task. The thing is, when your business is small, and you start to hire your first few workers, their productivity will really have a large impact on your business. No matter how big you get down the road, who you hire first is very important. So, before bringing someone on board, you'll want to very carefully make sure that they are the best candidate for the job. We've already covered some of the character traits and intangibles to look for in worker, but with a list of qualifications in hand, where is the best place to look?

Family

Most of the online sellers and business owners that I talk with, struggle with outsourcing and delegation, because they lack trust. They struggle with the thought of someone, anyone, taking over a very important part of their business. What if they're horrible at the job? What if all of the time and energy spent training this person ends up not being worth it in the end? What if they end up costing more money than they make? What if they really like the business model and they end up quitting and becoming a direct competitor? What if they steal stuff?

Have you struggled with any of those objections/questions? I know that more than a couple of those thoughts have run through my head when I was just starting to expand. In fact, I still worry about the trustworthiness of my workers from time to time.

Since you can typically trust your family, they may be the best place to look to find your first hire. Don't let your judgment be clouded by bias or partiality, but instead, look at everyone in your immediate and extended family and try to determine if they would fit the criteria. You don't want to hire someone just because they are related to you, or because they are in a tough financial situation and need the money. Instead, you want to make sure that they have all of the general characteristics that will help the produce and then succeed in the business.

The worst thing that you can do when hiring is bring someone on board who is destined to fail. Not only do you suffer as a business owner, but they'll suffer, because they'll struggle and then fail to succeed. Really think about your family member and determine if you could really see them succeeding at the particular task.

If your 5' 5", 120 pound sister-in-law is looking for a stay-at-home job, before bringing her on as a Book Lister, be sure to consider the nature of the job. Will she have the willpower to work amidst all of the temptations and flexibility? Is she hardworking? Can she lift 40-50 pound boxes of books?

How about Grandma? Would she be a good fit as your newest Book Sourcer? Be sure to get an accurate assessment of her technological prowess. How well will she be able to operate a PDA and barcode scanner? Will she physically be able to negotiate a book sale with dozens of pounds of books in tow? Will she be able to source the bottom shelf? You don't want to set up expectations in your families' mind only for them to discover that they are unattainable.

When hiring family, you'll need to remember that there will be times when you'll need to put on your business owner hat. Just like all of your others workers, you'll need to always be offering tons of encouragement, but at the same time, you will need to be critical. If they are doing something wrong, you'll need to offer your gentle, yet firm, correction. Just be sure that if you're hiring a family member that you make sure that a "manager to employee relationship "would fit the current dynamic of the relationship.

Friends

We have had our most success hiring friends. It seems like the business dynamic has worked well in this context. The reason it has been easier is that we have been able to accurately, for the most part, assess the candidate's work ethic and loyalty before we even suggest the job to them. In fact, we had already decided that we wanted to hire one of our Sourcers before he even knew that the position and opportunity existed. Here's how it works. Since we compensate so well, it's easy for us to lure someone into our company, because there are so many perks to working for us (high pay, lots of flexibility, and tons of room for growth).

We don't have to beg anyone to work for us; in fact, we can go out, find candidates for the position, even if they are already employed and then we can sell them on the job. Just like with hiring family, there may be a temptation to be biased and partial with your assessment of their skills. If you have a heart, it's hard to see someone you care about struggle financially, but don't let this be the determining factor as to whether or not you hire someone. It is imperative for you and for them that this person, if given the job, has the characteristics necessary to succeed.

Be sure to ask yourself the same questions: Is this person primed and ready to work hard, or would they be more of a "project employee"? Does this friend of mine have all of the intangibles necessary to succeed? Is this someone that I can be open and honest with?

After running your friend through the ringer, if they come out intact, then I would recommend seriously considering them for the job.

Strangers

I arranged a meeting with my Book Sales Manager, and since I was a bit early, I met him at a thrift store (he was just wrapping up). With a cart full of books already, he was working on his last couple of shelves. As we were chatting, a 20-something year-old stopped by to ask what we were doing. He seemed very interested in the business. In fact, he was so interested he asked if there were any positions available (I like that). Andrew, my manager (and brother-in-law) swapped numbers with the guy and said that he would be happy to meet to discuss the possibility of working for us as a Sourcer.

As it turns out, this perfect stranger morphed into one of our best Book Sourcers. Does that make you nervous, the idea handing the keys of a part of your business over to a perfect stranger? There are some helpful ways to alleviate some of these concerns. Make sure that you have a thorough well-thought-through interview process. Be sure to ask him or her all of the questions necessary to really get to know them and what drives them. After you've vetted him with a series of questions then you can put him or her on some sort of trial run to see how they do. Not only is it important for you to have confidence in their ability, but it is also crucial that they like the job.

I'll stress it again. If you follow my compensation plan, you should be on the lookout for highly qualified individuals. These positions offer a lot of perks and should be used to attract top talent.

Should You Have Your Workers Sign a Non-Compete Agreement?

We don't have our people sign non-compete agreements. A non-compete clause/agreement (NCC) is *"a term used in contract law under which one party (usually an employee) agrees not to enter into or start a similar profession or trade in competition against another party (usually the employer)."* One of the big fears that most online sellers have, when it comes to hiring help, is that all of the secrets of their business will be exposed and could potentially be used against them. What would stop a new worker from starting their own company and following our same business model? Both our Retail Sourcers and our Book Sourcers have access to a lot of profitable information; shouldn't we be worried?

First off, from the information that I've gathered, non-compete agreements are very hard to hold up in court. Regardless, I have no desire to get into litigation, especially over book selling. I would rather spend my time and money on building our business than squabbling in court. If one of our Book Sourcers defected, we may be slightly frustrated, but we would get over it pretty quickly. So, it really all boils down to a gentleman's agreement based on mutual trust. We ask all of our people to refrain from selling on Amazon while they are working for us. We also ask that our Book Sourcers refrain from using our scanning devices to buy their own inventory. But, I'm really not worried and this is why:

1) **Our Book-Manager, Book Sourcers, and Book Listers are compensated well, which means that they're happy.** We also go out of our way to ensure that they are recognized for their hard work in other ways. We try hard to ensure that they have no reason to leave, but every reason to stay. Also, if we have treated our workers well, and they are decent people, they wouldn't want to hurt our business by going into competition with us. We should try hard to earn the trust and admiration of those whom we employ. If we are successful, I'm confident we don't have to worry about being "stabbed in the back."

2) **It would take a significant investment for these people to start their own book-selling or retail arbitrage business**, that is, "significant" for most people these days. According to a recent article that was published on the Fox Business website, "The typical American isn't saving anything, according to a new survey." The article goes on to say that the average American has $668 left over each month after paying their bills, but most of this money is spent on luxury items or consumable products and not put into savings. This lack of savings really prevents people from taking what they learn about our business and applying it for themselves.

3) **Finally, most people are not entrepreneurial in heart & mind**. They aren't looking, and therefore seeing, the business opportunities that we do. I think back to the number of jobs that I have held over the years, and I never did any calculations as to how much money my employer was making off me. At the time, the whole idea of running a business seemed so confusing and complex. I was much more focused on the task at hand and on what I was looking forward to doing as soon as I got off work. People like a regular, dependable source of income, so the majority of people will have no desire to steal your business.

But this is my opinion. If you'd like to move ahead with a NCC, go for it. The beauty of being an entrepreneur is that you don't have to play by anyone else's rules. Maybe a solid NCC would be a good deterrent for potential defectors?

All-in-all, I care about the people who work for me, and I want them to succeed in big ways. So, the idea of them going into competition with my business is sort of bitter-sweet. On the one hand, I would be slightly annoyed that I had a new direct competitor, but at the same time, this person, who I care about, is starting their own business. This is a good thing! I would be happy that they decided to take the big leap into business ownership from "Employee" to the "Self-Employed."

Step #1 Acquire a Barcode Scanner
Step #2 Outsource With FBA
Step #3 Establish Book-buying Criteria
Step #4 Locate and Research Local Thrift-stores
Step #5 Do Some Scanning Yourself
Step #6 Prep., List, Pack and Document
Step #7 Establish How Your People Will Pay and Be Paid
Step #8 Hire Top Talent

Step # 9 Set Up Inventory Management Systems

"Stop chasing skills and start building systems. Learn to outsource work to the highest performing and lowest price option. People with skills work for rich people with ideas."
Jim Cockrum, on his blog at jimcockrum.com

"The way to wealth, if you desire it, is as plain as the way to market. It depends chiefly on two words: industry and frugality that is waste neither time nor money, but make the best use of both."
Benjamin Franklin

After you have gathered all of the equipment, established a solid book-sourcing criteria, mapped out a battle plan to tackle local thrift-stores, become comfortable at scanning and listing so that you could teach others, hired some top-talent and figured out how you are going to pay them, next you'll need to invest in a re-pricing program and think through ways to keep your seller metrics up and your customers happy. Maybe you're curious why this particular task has earned its own step. In my estimation, there are at least four good reasons why you should purchase and implement re-pricing software for your book selling business. But, before we get into those reasons, I'll explain to you what re-pricing software is.

Re-pricing Software

It is very important that your books are priced competitively, or else you could miss out on crucial sales. It's one thing to price your books accurately when listing, but it's another to ensure that they maintain their competitive price. If your book continues to be undercut in price then your copy could get buried which could lead to missed sales, sometimes only for a few pennies. Also, there have been many instances, in the history of our book selling business, in which books were re-priced up, which means that their prices were increased to meet the competition and then sold at a higher cost (which is great!). Either way it is important for your book-selling business to have a system that automatically maximizes profitability and sales. One very important solution to helping this along is a solid re-pricing program.

For books, we currently subscribe to a company called RePriceIt (www.repriceit.com). You pay monthly, starting at around $10/month, for this program (price is determined on how many individual items that you have listed that you would like to be tracked and re-priced), and this company will make sure that you're prices remain competitive, based solely on your re-pricing criteria. You can customize your criteria in a number of ways, including: a minimum and maximum allowable price, how our items should be re-priced according to competition, how aggressively we would like to pursue the "Buy Box", and how many times we would like to re-price our inventory per day, week or month. Just to name a few of the many options.

If you are interested in taking a look at my re-pricing criteria, click on this link: http://profitsourcing.com/blog/used-book-repricing-criteria

Our re-price software re-prices all of our books once per day, which we feel is a good amount of re-pricing to ensure that our books are in a good position to sell. If you are interested in looking into re-pricing options, be sure to do some research of your own. Other companies to consider, besides RePriceIt would include, but are not be limited to:

www.appeagle.com
www.teikametrics.com
www.feedvisor.com

Speeds Up the Listing Process

If you want your Book-Lister to price the books as he or she goes, it would add a significant amount of time per book listed. Choosing an accurate price can be a little tricky and would definitely take some extra training. There are lots of criteria to consider when choosing a competitive price and we do a lot of re-pricing by hand for the more expensive, non-book, retail items that we sell on Amazon. But since books are generally so cheap to acquire we have determined that they would be great candidates for this type of automation. It seems like it would be logical to consider outsourcing this a very important step in the automated book-selling process to automate re-pricing option.

Also, if you plan on using a re-pricer for price adjustments after the book has been listed, you shouldn't even bother having your Book-Lister price at all. Our books are all automatically listed at $400 so that some of the higher priced textbooks don't get sold before the re-pricing software has a chance to kick in, but the very next day they are all adjusted to meet the going rate.

With over 16,500 books currently active on Amazon, it would be very time-consuming to go through each listing to ensure that all of our books are priced properly. With programs such as this one, we can better utilize our time and focus our limited attention on the areas of our business that need our attention the most.

Customer Feedback Management

Just like in any business, it is very important to make sure that all of your customers are happy. Even if you plan on selling all of your items FBA, you'll need to be ready to deal out some amazing customer service at a moment's notice. Although Amazon will do all that they can within their power to make the customer happy, if they still end up leaving negative feedback, it's on you to make it right.

There are four reasons Amazon will remove negative feedback. So before you move forward, you'll want to check to see if the negative feedback: 1) is a product review, 2) is a fulfillment related issue (if sold via FBA), 3) includes seller-specific, personally identifiable information, including e-mail addresses, full names, or telephone numbers and/or 4) includes words commonly understood to be obscene or profane. For any of these reasons, Amazon will remove the negative feedback without you having to contact the customer.

Product Reviews

From time to time, the Amazon customer will get confused and will leave their product review in the area that is designated for buyer feedback. So, instead of commenting on your super-fast shipping, production condition, and packaging, they are commenting on the pros and cons of the actual product. We are basically book distributors. We provide new and used copies of the books that our Amazon customers are looking for. We, in no way shape or form, endorse all of the content in every book that we sell; that would be crazy. So, if you find yourself with some negative feedback in the comments section, and they clearly are upset about what the book has to say and not about anything that you would be culpable. Be sure to contact Amazon right away to have it removed.

Fulfillment Related Issues for FBA Sellers

If you sell books via FBA, occasionally you'll get some negative feedback that will have to do with problems on Amazon's end. This would include a book arriving to the customer later than promised or in damage condition (the box and the book). If this happens, be sure to request that this feedback be removed for "Fulfillment Related Comments".

Instead of removing feedback that is fulfillment related, they will cross it out and write:

This item was fulfilled by Amazon, and we take responsibility for this fulfillment experience.

The negative feedback will still be visible on your feedback page, but it will not negatively affect your seller metrics (which is the most important thing).

Personal Information

Amazon wants to protect your private information, so if one of your customers puts any personally identifiable information, which includes your email, address, full name, and/or phone number, Amazon will happily delete it. We have over 1,000 feedback ratings and I can't think of one instance where personal information was shared, but it's still good to be mindful of this, just in case it does happen.

Confusing or Profane Language

If you can't understand what the customer is trying to say and/or they are using foul language, Amazon says that they will delete it, since this clearly violates Amazon's Terms and Conditions.

So, if you run across negative feedback that falls into any of these categories, be sure to get it removed. For all other negative feedback, you'll need to put on your customer service hat.

Here's my strategy for turning a negative customer experience into a positive one: 1) admit ownership, 2) go above and beyond to make things right, and 3) ask nicely for action.

Admit Ownership of the Problem

Say you're sorry. I'll share with you my form letter in a moment, but sometimes our customers are most hurt because they feel like they have been taken advantage of, and you can really sense this in their comments. Therefore, sometimes all it takes is a heart-filled apology to turn things around. Even if I don't think that the whole ordeal is my fault, I'll still claim ownership, because the customer is always right (even when they're wrong). I'll give them the benefit of the doubt. If they say, "I'm angry because this book was filled with highlighting even though it was supposed to be in Used Very Good condition," I'll just go ahead and assume that I made a listing error.

If they claim that the book has more wear than it should, I'll just assume that I didn't pack the shipping box well enough to protect the books on their way to the fulfillment centers.

Go Above and Beyond

In addition to saying I'm sorry, I will go above and beyond to ensure that the customer is happy. 99% of the time this means that I will: 1) take full ownership, and 2) offer them a full refund. Because I really want them to be happy, I will give them a refund and let them keep the book. This over-the-top move has really led to some extremely satisfied customers. But, I don't stop there...

Ask Nicely for Action

Now that they have been blown away by some pretty solid customer service, I will ask them very nicely to consider removing their negative feedback. For most customers, this is asking a lot of them. Even though I supply the link for them to use to access and delete their feedback, this does require a few steps. It is an inconvenience; therefore, I think that it is important to really wow them into taking action.

My Feedback Removal Template

I have found over a 90% success rate getting negative feedback removed, and I simply take the steps mentioned and send the customer this form letter:

Mr./Mrs. _____ ,

I apologize for the condition of the item that you received from us. We always work very hard to ensure that the books that we list are accurately represented online. This was definitely an oversight on our part. I have gone ahead and have issued you a full refund for your purchase. Please, keep the book. We wouldn't want you to be inconvenienced any further. If you are satisfied with this resolution, would you please remove your negative feedback from our account? Negative customer experiences have a very real impact on our business. As a small family owned and operated online company, we strive to offer the Amazon marketplace the integrity and honesty it deserves. Thank you for your patience & understanding.

Click on this link to access completed feedback:
https://www.amazon.com/gp/feedback/leave-consolidated-feedback.html?ie=UTF8&isCBA&marketplaceID=ATVPDKIKX0DER&mode=submitted&orderID&ref_=cfb_el_su

Bryan Young
Owner

Buyers have 60 days to remove negative feedback

The Importance of Having Good Seller Metrics

Lately, I have been seeing a lot of Amazon sellers have their selling accounts suspended. Sometimes, it seems that this happens as a result of a glitch in the system, but oftentimes Amazon suspends a seller due to not taking care of their customers. Doing whatever you can to make the customer happy is not only good business, but it can help avoid getting your selling account shut down.

Your standing with Amazon is based on these performance metrics:

- Order Defect Rate (Negative Feedback)
- Cancellation Rate
- Late Shipment Rate
- Policy Violation
- On-Time Delivery
- Contact Response Time

If 100% of your inventory is FBA, then you really will only need to worry about your Order Defect Rate, which ultimately is tied to your overall seller feedback. My advice is to go all out to ensure that your customers will only have nice things to say about you and your business!

Should We Actively Pursue Positive Feedback From Our Customers?

There are some online sellers that spend time and money soliciting positive feedback. You can either email each and every customer of personally, or you can pay to have it automatically done. For a couple of months, I tried out a company called Feedback Five. For about $10/month, they will automatically send your customers an email requesting positive feedback if they have been satisfied with their overall buying experience. They claim that only 10% of Amazon customers leave feedback (I think that it is WAY lower than that), and if you pay for their service, it will help you get more feedback quicker.

The problem that I ran into was that not only did I get a handful of positive feedback as a result of signing up, but I also got a flood of negative feedbacks to go with it! Of course, I want to do everything and anything to create a good buying experience for my customers, but there is some wisdom in those who say you should avoid "Stirring the pot."

My advice to you is that there's no rush to build up your feedback. If you have a healthy long-term vision for this business, you don't need to obsess about feedback. Just sell products and in the process of managing this business on a day-by-day basis, look to find ways to meet and, sometimes,

ProfitSourcing.com

exceed your customer's expectations and the positive feedback will come.

If you're still interested in automating the feedback solicitation process, here are some companies that you should consider:

www.feedbackgenius.com
www.feedbackfive.com
www.sellerlabs.com

What Size of an Inventory is a Good Size?

With our mix of books, we consistently sell about 15% of our inventory every month in the off-season (February through mid-August) and then our books sales jump quite a bit once book selling season hits (late August through January). Obviously, the size of your inventory and its diversity are going to play a role in sales percentages, but we consistently sell about 25% of our inventory during the bookselling season.

A good sized inventory, as defined by me, is one that is big enough to generate enough profit to: 1) reinvest money into new books, which will, at minimum, replace those that have sold, and 2) provide the extra profits necessary to pay yourself.

Unfortunately, there isn't a magic number. But following those general percentages, you'll be able to visualize what size inventory will be necessary for you to achieve your goals.

I'll give you an example:
Let's say that you have 4,000 books in inventory. This would mean that you'd sell 600 a month during the off-season and 1,000 a month during the on-season. Using our criteria, our average sales price is about $14 per book, so if we applied that figure to our example on the off-months, we would bring in about $5,600 in gross revenue, and the on-months would gross $11,200. On a standard sized $14 book, sold FBA, we estimate that we'll make about $9.00 after Amazon fees and shipping. If we take into consideration the cost of the book and all other expenses (including, but not limited to, finders & listing fees, boxes, tape, membership fees, etc...), I would conservatively estimate that our net profit per book, on average, to

be about $5.

So according to these estimations, on the off-months with this size of inventory, we can expect to generate about $3,000 in profit, and that number would double to $5,000 in net profit during the bookselling season.

Of the $3,000 and $5,000 you would: 1) reinvest some of it into new inventory, and 2) pay yourself with the rest.

Just keep in mind that these numbers are very rough estimates and are not taking into consideration a variety of factors, such as the new inventory that's coming in every week along with the unique make up of your own inventory. But, I hope that these general figures will help you map out some goals for your business.

Step #1 Acquire a Barcode Scanner
Step #2 Outsource With FBA
Step #3 Establish Book-buying Criteria
Step #4 Locate and Research Local Thrift-stores
Step #5 Do Some Scanning Yourself
Step #6 Prep., List, Pack and Document
Step #7 Establish How Your People Will Pay and Be Paid
Step #8 Hire Top Talent
Step #9 Invest in Re-pricing Software

Step #10 Expand Your Entrepreneurial Mind

"What's my biggest motivation? Just to keep challenging myself. I see life almost like one long University education that I never had. Everyday I'm learning something new."
Richard Branson

The final step in setting yourself on the path to passive income success is to start thinking like an entrepreneur. My advice is to read lots and lots of books on business-building and entrepreneurialism, read blog posts, subscribe to podcasts, watch webinars, go to conferences, and don't just limit them to the online selling niche. Also, equally important, is to network with other online sellers. I have acquired a wealth of knowledge simply by being active on the various online selling forums. If you're not already in a mastermind group, join one. I started a small private mastermind group last year and the ideas, encouragement and feedback that I get from this group has been priceless. A mastermind group is a group of like-minded entrepreneurs that are committed to helping each other succeed. The beauty of a mastermind group is that participants raise the bar by challenging each other to create and implement goals. It's such a great support system for growing businesses.

I know that it has been easier for me to see outsourcing, and business building opportunities in my Amazon business than it has been for other sellers because I always look for ways to feed my mind with solid entrepreneurial advice, and I highly advise you to do the same. Here are some resources that have had a big impact on the formations of my business mindset:

Books
(The books in bold are "Must Reads")

Outliers, by Malcolm Gladwell
The Tipping Point, by Malcolm Gladwell
Crush it!, by Gary Vaynerchuk
The Thank You Economy, by Gary Vaynerchuk
Entreleadership, by Dave Ramsey
Tribes, by Seth Godin
The Purple Cow, by Seth Godin
Permission Marketing, by Seth Godin
How to Develop Self Confidence and Influence People by Public Speaking, by Dale Carnegie
How to Win Friends and Influence People, by Dale Carnegie

Silent Sales Machine, by Jim Cockrum
Rich Dad, Poor Dad, by Robert Kiyosaki
Cashflow Quadrant, by Robert Kiyosaki
The 4 Hour Work Week, by Tim Ferris
Multiple Streams of Income, by Robert Allen
Trump: The Art of the Deal, by Donald Trump
The Long Tail, by Chris Anderson
How to Sell at Margins Higher Than Your Competitors, by Lawrence Steinmetz
Visioneering, Andy Stanley
The Millionaire Mind, by Thomas Stanely
Money, Possessions and Eternity, by Randy Alcorn
The Treasure Principle, by Randy Alcorn
Winning, by Jack Welch
E-Myth Mastery, by Michael Gerber

The crazy thing is that I've read all of these books and many more over the course of the last couple of years. How do I find the time to read all of these books? You may be asking this question. I cut out much of the unproductive entertainment that I once had in my life. Chelsea and I decide to not have television be a regular influence in our lives and in the lives of our children. We have a projector in the basement for an occasional show (Downtown Abbey, for instance) or movie. But, seeing the projector on, is not a regular occurrence, especially in the summer.

Instead we would rather be taking advantage of this "Information Age" that we live in and filling our minds with things that are going to help us be more productive, as well as give us more freedom and flexibility to spend time with each other.

Podcasts

I have only, over the last few months, started to seriously listen to podcasts online, but the shows that I've found have already had a major impact on my entrepreneurial mindset and my business. My all time favorite show is **Pat Flynn's Smart Passive Income** Radio Show (can be found at the Apple Podcast Store). If you would like to check out his podcast show and some of the other resources that he gives away for free, check out his website at www.smartpassiveincome.com. If you're worried about finding time to listen to a podcast, don't. I work from home with (now 7) young children and yet I still find an hour each day, on average, to listen to podcasts. It's easy. Just download a show and enjoy it while you get work done around the house, or while you are driving, shopping, or cooking. I look forward to listening to Pat's shows so much, that I sort of look forward to doing housework!

Other podcasts that I've enjoyed include The Tim Ferris Show, by Tim Ferris of course. If you don't know who he is you should spend a little time getting to know him. He's the author of the book *The Four Hour Work Week*. You can also find his podcast on iTunes or at his website directly at www.fourhourworkweek.com.

Also, check out the Dave Ramsey Show, for great insight on what it means to be a successful entrepreneur and leader. His show can be found on iTunes or at www.daveramsey.com/entreleadership/podcast.

I also really enjoy the James Altucher Show, Seth Godin's Startup School & Build Your Tribe.

I'm sure that there are many more that I haven't even been exposed to, but these are the excellent ones that I make sure to keep up on.

Magazines

Do they still even print magazines? Yes, they do. There are a couple of magazines that I would highly recommend that you subscribe to:

Success Magazine – This magazine comes with 2-3 interviews on an audio CD every month and is filled with great info.
The Harvard Business Review – This magazine comes out quarterly and is filled with solid entrepreneurial ideas.

Other Online Resources

Check out all of the other resources that are available online. We live in what's considered a rural area, and unfortunately, we don't have very fast or reliable internet. As a result, we haven't been able to take advantage of all of the free webinars and video conferencing shows that are out there. If your town has technology from the 21st century, be on the lookout for some excellent video based resources.

Also, there are some solid courses and training materials available for purchase. Although there is an abundance of material out there that can be read for free if you are a just getting started selling on Amazon or even if you are a seasoned online seller, I would highly recommend looking into our Book Flipping online Training Course (Sign up for information by going to https://profitsourcing.leadpages.co/thankyou/). This course not only walks you through the basics of online selling it also lays out all of my practical entrepreneurial tactics and strategies so that you can start and then fully outsource your own book selling business (more on this later).

Conferences

I highly recommend going to live conferences. It's a great way to get some solid information and encouragement for the presentations, but it is also an incredible networking opportunity. Last year I went to two different business conferences and both of them had a big impact on the growth and direction of our business. Remember that educational opportunities, such as live conferences, can be written off as a business expense.

Stay tuned for more information about an up-and-coming "Book-Flipping Conference" – to ensure that you're in the loop be sure to sign-up by going to this link: https://profitsourcing.leadpages.co/thankyou/

In the book *E-Myth Revised*, Gerber writes, "As a result of these experiences(Gerber's experiences helping business owners realize their own potential), I've come to the conclusion that each of us is born with an inherent impulse, a creative center, which, when cultivated through disciplined learning and practice, can produce works in the world that defy the imagination, entrepreneurial works. These are works of the entrepreneurial kind." Don't buy into the myth that entrepreneurs are born and not made. Gerber actually thinks that we all have the innate qualities of an entrepreneur, and through hard work and hustle, all of us can pursue the entrepreneurial path to success. If you want to be an entrepreneur, but aren't one yet, it's probably because you haven't worked very hard at it.

Ask yourself these questions:

How bad do I really want to build a successful business?

Do I want it bad enough to turn the T.V. Off?

Do I want it so bad that I'll get up at 5:00am every morning to ensure that it happens?

Am I willing to cultivate a lifestyle of education, redeeming every opportunity possible to broaden my entrepreneurial mind?

What Gerber writes in his book along with many other writers of our day is that you can be successful in business if you want it bad enough. The determining factor to your success is you. That's pretty empowering stuff, isn't it?

I could go on and on about all of the different ways you could enrich and grow your entrepreneurial mind but I don't want to get too carried away. Don't buy into the myth that you weren't born with the DNA of a successful business owner. Don't sell yourself short. With disciplined learning and practice, you can become an entrepreneur. It will take time and effort, like anything else worth learning, but will be completely worth it.

What about Health Care?

One of the typical objections that I get to entrepreneurialism of any kind is, "Yeah, that's sounds great, but then I won't have health care coverage." The thing that apparently is holding so many people back from achieving their dreams, from killing the job, and getting out there to build a business on their own is a lack of health insurance. That is such a shame.

The good news is that, now, there are more possibilities than ever to acquire comprehensive healthcare at an affordable rate.

First off, if you want to think like an entrepreneur, your approach to any of the roadblocks along the way should be, "How can I overcome this obstacle?" You should always be approaching things with a solutions-based mind-set. So, with that in mind, we should be asking ourselves, "How can I find affordable healthcare coverage?"

We are a part of a medical sharing organization, which is different than your typical heath insurance company. Every month, we pay Samaritan's Ministries, on average, $375 to fully cover our family of 9, and the handful of times that we have had to file a claim, the whole process worked seamlessly. I put together a short nine-minute video on this very topic on the website if you're interested:

http://profitsourcing.com/uncategorized/health-care-coverage-for-the-online-entrepreneur

Here's a list of some reputable Medical Sharing companies that I recommend you look into if you are in need of health insurance:

Samaritan Ministries
Christian Healthcare Ministries
Medi-Share

If you'd like to shop some traditional health insurance plans, I'd recommend that you head over to www.eHealthInsurance.com to get a quick estimate from a handful of the biggest insurance companies in the U.S.

Conclusion

"The best way to predict the future is to create it."
Peter Drucker, writer.

So there you have it. I've given you the keys to running a profitable, automated used book selling business. Hopefully you have been inspired by all of the outsourcing principles that I've discussed as well as found value in the various ways that I demonstrated their application.

Spending time with my family is of utmost importance and what this book selling business has done, is that it has given me the freedom and flexibility to do just that. I get to share three meals with my family every, single day. How cool is that? **What's your "Why"?** Is it family? Is it a noble cause? Is it travel? Let the things that matter most to you besides money, motivate your entrepreneurial endeavors and I know that you can succeed.

Don't be afraid to go against the grain. My wife and I, with six kids, left comfortable jobs at the Mayo Clinic to pursue the dream of a home-based business and people thought we were crazy! They couldn't wrap their minds around all of the security that we were giving up to pursue online sales. "How are you going to pay for health insurance?" or "You know that most businesses fail. What happens if yours fails?" they'd ask. Total failure was not an option for us. We made it one of our goals to prove these naysayers wrong. Do you have that kind of gumption?

The used book market on Amazon is filled with opportunity, because people still buy physical copies of non-fiction books even though we have seen the market flooded with eBooks over the last couple of years. I understand that this may all change in the future. I'm sure that technology will make it easier to use eBooks as reference books but for the time being, there are nice profits to be made in the non-fiction book selling business.

Never in the history of the world has a culture experienced the technology that we all have available at our fingertips. While most people are using it to play Bejeweled, let's use it to build a 7-figure online sales company! Technology is a vehicle to help you scale your business, and it takes nearly all of the guess work out of sourcing. Take the time to **check out tech companies such as ASellerTool and NeatOScan** to see if their services could benefit your business.

Fulfillment and distribution centers used to only be accessible to the very large corporations throughout the U.S. Now, with **Amazon FBA**, we can all logistically compete with the big dogs! We have access to a state of the art, world-class network of fulfillment centers that not only allows us to compete with the big companies around the world but very often gives us a competitive advantage.

Determine your buying criteria and simplify it. Not only will this exercise help you outsource portions of your book-sourcing business, but it will also bring clarity and focus to what you're really looking for in a product. Don't over complicate things for your Book Sourcers since it may really bog down the whole process.

Prepare your business for success through proper planning. For book-sourcing, this looks like mapping out the city and really systematizing the whole book sourcing process. Put your Book Sourcers in a position to succeed. Before you send out your army of shoppers to all of the thrift-stores in town, do a little scanning yourself and let your excitement for the "hunt" stir up excitement in those you will have working for you. Also, I recommend you put together some of your own shipments, from start to finish, so that you can have a good handle on the process.

What's really exciting is that this whole bookselling operation can be set up for under $600! I told that to an old farmer once. He was thinking about buying and selling some books on the side for some extra money. Also, it would be a way for him to spend some productive time with his college-aged girls when they came home from school in the summer. He said, "$600 is great! It's much cheaper than starting a cow business!" He then went on to tell a story of how he spent over $900 on one cow only to have it die on him within the first year!

This business can provide some great paying jobs for people who need them. It feels good to create jobs. Have you ever known someone who was hard-up for work? Someone whom you would have loved to help out, but couldn't? With this business you can! The large "Profit Cushion" that is found in used books will allow you to create jobs and compensate your workers very well.

Be sure to fill your team with the best talent possible. Don't be afraid to hire people who are smarter than you. Hire people who are strong in the areas that you're weak in and then get out of the way.

Once you're book inventory gets to over 1,000 titles you should consider an automatic re-pricer. Subscribing to a re-pricing company, such as Repriceit, is another easy way to automate your business. You can have the re-pricer, re-price your book every hour if you'd like, there's no way that you could do that manually with a large inventory, even if you tried your hardest!

Finally, you need to work on building and expanding an entrepreneurial mindset. If you're like most people everything that has been ingrained in you thus far runs in opposition to the mindset that you need to succeed in business. If you don't have wise business-minded people nearby, the next best thing is to read their books. Also, listen to podcasts, such as the ones that I suggested, or do a search for resources yourself.

I hope this book has inspired you to look beyond the walls of the "Self-Employed" online businesses, to see the possibilities that are there for a well-designed business system. An automated book-selling business is not only a great way to make some passive income, as I have demonstrated, but it is a great way to get freedom in your life. Figure out your "Why". Figure out what is most important to you and look for ways to maximize that. The "Why" will be the key to motivating your business to success.

So, what are you waiting for? Don't let this opportunity pass you by! Start small. Take risks. Embrace failure.

Thank you for taking the time to read my book, if there is anything that I can do to help you successfully get your online business off the ground, please don't hesitate to ask. Helping others start and grow their Amazon business has been a passion and a joy of mine for a long time.

I will continually be adding new content related to online selling to my website, www.profitsourcing.com. Be sure to check it out if you haven't already. Also, if you'd like to discuss book selling, or if you just need some guidance I would be happy to help. Send me a personal email at bryanrobertyoung@gmail.com

Bonus Chapter

The Book Sourcing Manual

In this training manual we will cover the basics of Book Sourcing. With the information you will learn in this guide, you will have all of the knowledge necessary to get started and succeed as a Book Sourcer.

ProfitSourcing.com
Table of Contents

1

Introduction

What is Book Sourcing?
It is the process locating and buying books that will later be sold online.

Where does Book Sourcing take place?
There are so many sources for used books that the opportunities are overwhelming. In this guide we will cover some of these sources but as you gain experience in this position be sure to keep your eyes open for new opportunities.

Why Are There Book Sourcers?
You may be wondering, 'why does a position like this even exist?' That's a great question. People, throughout the world, still enjoy buying physical books. In fact, over the last few months the market has seen a decline in eBook sales and a boost in physical book sales. Often times when the original consumer of a book is finished reading it they don't really know what to do with it. Many people will donate them to a local non-profit to be sold, and others will have sales. Depending on the nature of the book, it can sometimes be really difficult to find someone who want to buy the books that you're looking to get rid of.

The thrift stores and library sales are unfortunately the first and last stop for many of these books. Books that don't sell here often times are sent off to the dump. Since books have a glue binding many cannot be recycled, very efficiently, without a book-unbinding machine, therefore most of them are thrown away.

Here's where we come in. We look for books, utilizing technologies that have unrealized demand around the world, buy them and then meet that demand. That copy of <u>One Souls Journey: To Find Streams of Water in the Desert</u> by Cashel Weiler, may not have found any takers at the local thrift-store but there are people online waiting to buy the first copy that comes available. We sold our copy just a few days ago and here's the feedback we received:

As online booksellers we provide value. We rescue the books that are on death-row, pluck them from the hands of the garbage man, and re-circulate them back into the world. It truly is a win-win-win-win-win business; the customer wins because they finally found an affordable copy of the book they have been looking for, the thrift-store or book sale wins because they are able to sell their book to raise money for their cause, Amazon wins because they are able to continue to serve their customers world-wide, our company wins because not only are we able to meet needs and provide value but we can make a nice profit, and finally the whole of society wins because we are recirculating the valuable information found in these books as well as putting a stop to needless waste in our nation's landfills.

Equipment & Technology

We live in age of ever advancing technology. In the past for an individual to successfully source books they would need to have an extensive knowledge of the book selling marketplace to figure out which books were worth buying and which ones were not. This knowledge of course would take years to acquire and still it wouldn't be exhaustive. Because there are tens of millions of titles being sold on Amazon there would be no way to know the current price and rank of each and every book. This is where technology comes in.

With the Amazon book database in hand we are able to rapidly determine the value of books without having to rely solely on intuition. By simply scanning the book's barcode or entering the ISBN we can find out what the books going rate on Amazon is and then we can make an informed purchasing decision. When it comes to book sourcing tools here are the options:

1. PDA (Personal Digital Assistant) + Socket Laser Scanner
2. Smart Phone + FBAScan App
3. Smart Phone + Other Scanning App

PDA + Socket Laser Scanner

The PDA was a piece of technology that was popular in the mid-nineties. Everything that a PDA could do has been replaced by smart phones. But, the PDA still works great for book sourcing and is our favorite of the three options.

Here's how it works, you buy an old PDA, either from ASellerTool or on eBay, you pay to have it loaded with the Amazon database, and then you use it to rapidly determine a books value. This can be done by scanning the barcode on the back of the book with a laser scanner. On the Dell Axim x51 PDA there's a little slot into which an SD Socket scanner fits perfectly. At the press of a button you are able to scan a barcode and pull up a book listing on the PDA to quickly determine if a book meets your buying criteria. All of the relevant information is displayed on one screen, at a glance you'll be able to see what the book is currently selling for in both new and used conditions, how many offers there are on the listing, and what the sales rank is. This will give you all of the information necessary to make a purchasing decision based on the criteria (more on this later).

What about books that don't have barcodes? You can also enter UPCs & ISBNs manually into the PDA which takes a bit longer but will help make sure that you don't skip over any books.

The Pros of the PDA Method of Scanning:

One of the main benefits of the PDA scanning method is that you don't have to rely on cell phone signal or Wi-Fi to source books. Since all of the relevant data has been uploaded to the memory card that's in the device you can scan away without having to worry about finding a signal. Because the PDA program only gives you the information that you need (title, rank & offers) there's no loading. After scanning a barcode all of the relevant info shoots up on the screen, which means that once you get comfortable with the layout you'll be able to scan books very fast. Also using PDAs mean that you don't need to have a phone with app capabilities to source books. Everything that you need to be a successful Book Sourcer is included in the PDA sourcing package.

The Cons of the PDA Method of Scanning:

PDAs are no longer in production, which means that there may come a time in the not-to-distant future when you are no longer able to purchase one. One of the other notable cons is that the information on the PDA is only as current as the last time that the database was updated. If you don't regularly update your database you could be working with stale information. Regardless, there is always a delay after you source books. The books need to be prepped and shipped off to Amazon, and then need to be received and processed before they will be eventually for sale. Thus, even the live data methods, smartphones with sourcing apps and wifi or cell phone reception, have this drawback.

All-in-all we feel like the PDA method of Scanning is the best method, all things considered.

Smart Phone + FBAScan App

Our second favorite option would be using a smart phone and the FBAScan App. FBAScan is a program that was developed by ASellerTool, which is one of the few companies that provide PDA databases. The difference between FBAScan and other sourcing apps is that this one also has a database as a back-up just in case that there isn't any cell phone reception. To be able to use this scanning option you'll need a working smart phone with the capability to load this app plus about 2GB of free memory space for the Amazon database.

The Pros of Smart Phone + FBAScan App:

We really like the fact that the FBAScan App has a the Amazon database as a backup, just in case your Wi-Fi or cell phone reception runs out. This way you can look up book prices live occasionally. Other smart phone apps only have the online sourcing option which means that when the reception goes, so does your book scanning opportunities.

The Cons of Smart Phone + FBAScan App:

This option does have its drawbacks. You'll need to have the appropriate cell phone plus a substantial amount of space of the Amazon database. Plus, since you'll be scanning barcodes you'll need to buy a Bluetooth laser scanner to pair with your phone which could end up costing more than the whole PDA sourcing package on its own. You can use your smart phone camera to capture and evaluate barcodes but since your camera will need to spend a few moments focusing before it's able to snap the picture this could take a significant amount of time.

Overall, we like the Smart Phone + FBAScan option if you have the equipment required to use it to its full capability.

Smart Phone + Other Scanning App

The third and finally option, in our minds, is Smart Phone + Other Scanning App. Now there are quite a number of free and paid sourcing apps on the market that will work on Android and Apple phones. If you decide to go this route you'll need to have an app capable phone with a rear facing camera. You'll also need to have some sort of data feature activated on your cellphone plan to be able to utilize cell phone reception while you are out book sourcing.

The Pros of Smart Phone + Other Scanning App

This option is the cheapest of the three. If you already have the phone and the reception you can download a handful of apps for free. This means that if you'd like to try out the book sourcing business without investing in a ton of expensive equipment, you can. There are fantastic apps that cost money, either one time or monthly, to use but are totally worth it. Another important pro of this method is that like the FBAScan app you'll be able to use live data while you are sourcing. Although, we firmly believe that this shouldn't be the determining factor with whichever option you choose, since there will be significant lag time between the purchase and the book becoming active for sale on Amazon. It's a point worth considering.

The Cons of the Smart Phone + Other Scanning App

The drawbacks are that you'll need to have some sort of external Bluetooth laser scanner if you want to source books with any speed (and speed is key). These scanners are very nice, but they can get rather expensive. Sourcing books with this method will require that you have fast and consistent cell phone reception and Wi-Fi, which isn't always possible out in the field.

If you are just starting out and you'd like to try book sourcing without incurring too much cost, this is a good option. But, once you've decided that you would like to get serious about book sourcing, I would wholeheartedly recommend that you consider one of the first two options.

Now that you have the technology in hand now you'll need to understand which books to buy and which ones to pass on.

ProfitSourcing.com

Book Buying Criteria

Clear and Simple

Not every book that you scan will be worth reselling on Amazon, in fact most of the books that you scan will not be worth it. I would say that typically only 1 out of 10 are worth buying which is why speed is of the essence. The goal is to buy the books that have the highest likelihood of selling online. Although there is never a "sure thing", having a solid criteria is a step in the right direction. Here is our book buying criteria:

- Only buy books for $2 or less
- Only buy books that can be sold, in their current condition, for at least $10.95
- Only buy books with an Amazon rank of 1 – 5,000,000

That's it! Again, staying in those parameters doesn't guarantee a future sale but it will put our inventory in an excellent position to succeed. We typically don't want to buy books that will cost us more than $2 a piece, although there may be some exceptions to this rule. The other two criteria points can be determined using your scanning device. In the books current condition, can you sell it for $10.95 or more? If you answered yes to that question, does it have an Amazon rank under 5,000,000? If you answered yes to both of these questions and you can acquire that book for $2 or less than you should go ahead and buy it.

Once you get comfortable using the scanning technology, you'll be able to very rapidly determine if a particular book meets your criteria or not.

In addition to these three bullet points we also ask be mindful of these things:

- Does the title of the book you are scanning match the title on the PDA?
- Are there any pages missing?
- Is there excessive writing or highlighting? Does this obscure the text?
- Is the ethical nature of the book questionable?

- Is the book supposed to have a dust-jacket? Is it intact?
- Does the book promise any extras (DVD or CD)? Are they enclosed?
- Does the book come with an access code? Has it been opened/scratched/removed?

Although Amazon Rank is typically overlooked here are a few things to consider:

- Is the poor rank a reflection of a lack of supply?
- Is the poor rank a reflection of a lack of FBA sellers?
- According to your good judgment, is this book outdated, and unlikely to sell?

Once again, as you get comfortable scanning and evaluating books these criteria will be quickly deduced. Amazon requires that the books are complete (no missing pages) and that the marking can't be excessive to point that it obscures the text. Plus, it's important to note that if a book promises a Disc or Online Code that these should be intact. If they are missing we may still be able to resell the book but it would more than likely need to be sold in Acceptable condition. With some of these key extras missing, could the book be realistically sold for $10.95+? Probably not.

Also, we believe in only purchasing books that are ethically in line with our beliefs. Therefore, books of questionable ethical value should be avoided. If you would like us to elaborate on that a bit, let us know.

There will be some books that have a 5,000,000+ rank that may still be worth buying. When considering a book with a high rank ask yourself "Is the poor rank a reflection of a lack of supply?" Meaning, maybe the demand is there for a particular title, but since supply is low consumers haven't been able to purchase that particular title and therefore the sales rank shows it. Or, maybe the poor rank is a reflection of a lack of FBA (Fulfillment by Amazon) sellers? Sometimes our Amazon customers aren't willing to wait for a book that is Merchant Fulfilled (MF).

What is FBA and MF?

When a book is sold FBA that means that the book is being store at an Amazon fulfillment center pending sale. Once the book is sold on Amazon.com, the warehouse workers will locate the book and will send it directly to the customer. If there are any issues with the order Amazon will handle them all, since Amazon is fulfilling the order. Amazon will process all customer returns and adjustments.

Books that are MF, or Merchant Fulfilled, and shipped to the paying customer from the 3rd party seller (from their own home or warehouse). The MF seller, not Amazon, handles all customer service and returns if the need arises.

The big benefits to selling books FBA is that customers willing to pay a premium for books that are Prime Eligible and sometimes this premium will result in books being profitable enough to resell (whereas they might not be if sold MF). Amazon customers typically would rather 1) work with Amazon if there are any problems with their order, and 2) get their book within 2 days, guaranteed.

We sell all of our books FBA which means that when we are out sourcing books we can always assume that we will be able to sell a particular book for more money than our MF competition. Typically we sell our FBA books for $2-4 more than our comparable MF competition. Therefore, if you find a book in Used Very Good condition (more on this in a bit) and there's a copy that is being Merchant Fulfilled in that same condition for say $16.70, we would estimate that we could sell that same book FBA for at least $18.70. I'll get more into pricing in a moment.

Let's quickly walk through the book buying criteria so that you can grasp exactly what we are looking for in a book.

Book Buying Criteria in Action

Can the Book be bought for $2 or less?

It is very important that we keep the acquisition costs of books as low as possible. To ensure that we don't spend too much on books we have set the maximum cost for any book at $2. Not only is this going to ensure that the price we pay for our books is manageable but this should encourage those who perform out book sourcing to be on the lookout for good sales & deals. When sourcing books the first question that you should be asking yourself is, "Can I buy these books for $2 or less?"

Can The Book Be Sold For $10.95+?

The first thing that you need to do to determine if a book can be sold for $10.95+ is to figure out what condition it is in, in accordance with Amazon condition guidelines. A book's condition will fall into one of these categories:

- *New:* Just like it sounds. A brand-new, unused, unread copy in perfect condition. The dust cover and original protective wrapping, if any, are intact. All supplementary materials are included and all access codes for electronic material, if applicable, are valid and/or in working condition.

- *Used - Like New:* Dust cover is intact, with no nicks or tears. Spine has no signs of creasing. Pages are clean and not marred by notes or folds of any kind. May contain remainder marks on outside edges, which should be noted in listing comments.

- *Used - Very Good:* Pages and dust cover are intact and not marred by notes or highlighting. The spine is undamaged.

- *Used - Good:* All pages and cover are intact (including the dust cover, if applicable). Spine may show signs of wear. Pages may include limited notes and highlighting. May include "From the library of" labels.

- *Used - Acceptable:* All pages and the cover are intact, but the dust cover may be missing. Pages may include limited notes and highlighting, but the text cannot be obscured or unreadable.

- *Unacceptable:* Includes missing pages and obscured or unreadable text. We also do not permit the sale of advance reading copies, including uncorrected proofs, of in-print or not-yet-published books.

After you've determined the books condition, next you'll need to determine what the going rate on Amazon is. If, in the books current condition, you determine that we should be reasonably able to sell that book for at least $10.95 then you should go ahead and buy it. In the following chapter I will walk you through the entire evaluating process, so stay tuned.

Does the Book Have an Amazon Sales Rank of 5,000,000 or less?

Our third and final question is very straight forward. Does your book have a rank of 5 million or better? Sales rank is simply a snap-shot in time. When you see the rank of a book you are seeing how this particular title stacks up against all of the other books that are available for sale on Amazon. The number basically represents how many copies of a particular book has sold over the last handful of hours in comparison to all of the other books that are selling. The higher the number the higher the likelihood that this book will sell for us.

If you read your layout and see that the rank is in these parameters, then you're good to go.

If you can answer yes to all three of these questions, I believe that you've found a winner! Next, I'd like to spend some time helping you familiarizing yourself with ASellerTool and their PDA program, as well as walk you through the Book Evaluating process...

Familiarizing Yourself with ASellerTool's PDA Program

A Progressive Look at the Book Sourcing Program

I'm going to walk you through the ASellerTool's PDA readout for a book I scanned. Let's say that you found this book on the shelf that is in Used-Very Good condition. It's a book that looks decent, the pages are relatively clean and crisp and as you quickly flip through the pages you notice that there isn't any highlighting or markings.

You scan the barcode on the back of the book with your laser scanner and this is the information/image that comes up on your PDA:

Let's start at the top.

1. This field will display the last barcode entered.

2. This field will display a shortened title for the current item.

3. This button opens up a keyboard display where you can manually input a barcode.

4. This field displays a **BUY** or **REJECT** indication. You can con figure this field using the **Criteria Group** and **Pricing Trigger** settings.

If this field is RED, as in the above example, the item is a **REJECT**.

If the field is GREEN, then the item is a **BUY**.

On a side note I don't recommend that you use the Buy/Reject triggers since there are so many variables that need to be considered and cannot be accurately condensed into the PDAs criteria. If you were sourcing books that all cost the same and were all in the same condition then this may work, otherwise it would be better for you to learn how to quickly read the screen and make a decision that way instead.

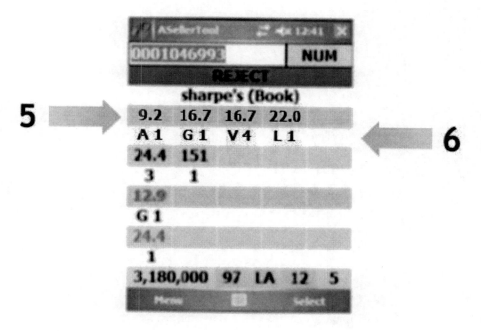

5. This field will show you the lowest used price, followed by up to 4 lowest used prices for the item. If you uncheck "Display FBA Offers Separately" in **Program Settings**, FBA prices will also be displayed in red.

6. This field displays conditions and numbers of offers in a used offers group.

Lettered abbreviations indicate the condition of a used item.

L = Like New

V = Very Good

G = Good

A = Acceptable

If you checked "Display number of Offers in Group" in **Program Settings**, then a number will appear next to the condition. The number will indicate number of offers in this group. If the letter/number appears pink, this means that there is more than one lowest price offer in this group.

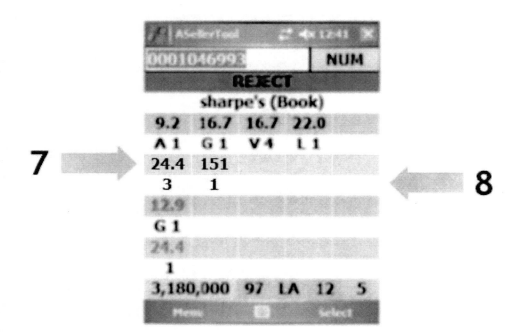

7. This field shows the lowest new price, followed by up to four of the lowest new prices in each group. If you uncheck "Display FBA Offers Separately" in **Program Settings**, FBA prices will appear in red in this field.

8. This field will display the number of offers in a new offers group.

If you checked "Display number of Offers in Group" in **Program Settings**, this row will be visible. The number will indicate the number of offers in this group. If the number in this field is pink it means there is more than one offer at the lowest price in this group.

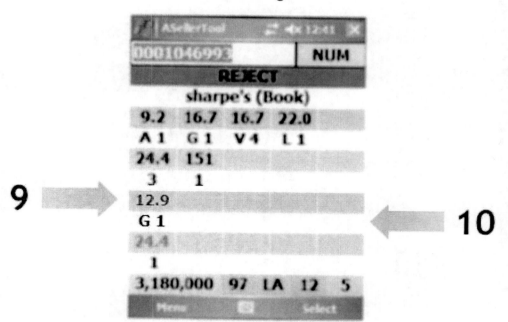

9. This field shows the used FBA prices. If you checked "Display FBA Offers Separately" in **Program Settings,** this row will show the FBA offers in red.

10. This field shows used conditions and number of offers in a used offers group for FBA offers.

Lettered abbreviations indicate the condition of a used item.

L = Like New

V = Very Good

G = Good

A = Acceptable

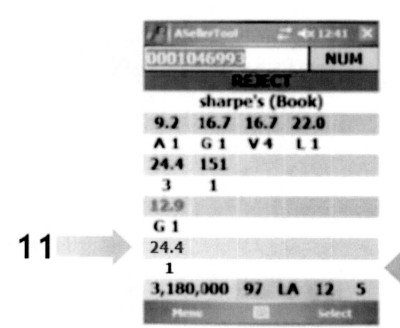

11. This field shows New FBA Prices. If you checked "Display FBA Offers Separately" in **Program Settings**, this row has the prices of new FBA offers displayed in red.

12. This field shows the number of offers in a new offers group for FBA offers see item eight above for more explanation on how this field works.

13. This field displays the Amazon sales rank of the item.

14. This area will show your PDA's remaining battery life, from 100% to 0.

15. This field displays the current pricing trigger.

16. This field displays the total number of used offers up to 255.

17. This field shows the total number of new offers up to 255.

To Buy or not to Buy?

Evaluating the Data

Based our criteria, if you found this particular book for less than $2 in Very Good condition **you should buy it**, and here's why:

The top 2 rows give you the used (green) and new (blue) Merchant Fulfilled prices. I already like what I'm seeing, this book is selling for a decent price amongst the MF sellers, which means that we should be able to command a very nice price for our FBA copy.

As you can see the lowest 4 used offers are (in the green horizontal column); $9.20, $16.70, $16.70 & $22.00.

Directly below these prices are their corresponding used condition and a number indicating quantity; 1 Acceptable, 1 Good, 4 Very Good and 1 Like New.

There are two New offers from Merchant Fulfilled sellers (prices are found in the blue horizontal column); $24.40 & $151.00.

Since these are New books directly below their price is just a number which indicates how many there are in stock, 3 @ $24.40 and 1 @ $151.00.

The next two colored rows are the used (green) and new (blue) Fulfillment by Amazon prices.

There is currently only one FBA seller selling this book used at $12.90 in Used Good condition. There is also only one FBA seller selling this book in New condition @ $24.40.

Estimating Price

To figure out if our book meets the estimated sale price criteria (which is $10.95 or more) we will use the information on this screen. When pricing a book go through these steps in order:

1. **Is there a comparable FBA price?** Meaning, is there an FBA seller who is selling the exact same book in the exact same condition already? If the answer is yes, then you will assume that you will be matching that price. So in our example above, if the book that we were looking at was in Used-Good condition I see that there is already an FBA seller selling that book for $12.90 in that condition. I'd anticipate matching that price and would move on to "Determining Rank". Since there are no FBA sellers selling this book in Used-Very Good condition we'll move on to the next step.

2. **What is this book being Merchant Fulfilled for in its comparable condition?** According to our PDA layout there is 4 copies being sold by a MF seller for a price of $16.70. Now, we could add $3 to the comparable MF copy and move on but there are a couple of other things to consider first.

| ASellerTool | | | ⇄ ◀× 12:41 | ✕ |

| 0001046993 | | NUM |

REJECT

sharpe's (Book)

9.2	16.7	16.7	22.0
A 1	G 1	V 4	L 1
24.4	151
3	1

12.9

G 1

24.4

1

| 3,180,000 | 97 | LA | 12 | 5 |

Menu   Select

Even though there are a limited number of FBA sellers selling this particular book, what are they selling for and how will our copy fit into the mix? As we noticed before there is a Used Good copy being sold for $12.90 and a New copy for $24.40. Since Used Very Good is better than Used Good but not as nice as a New copy, we should price accordingly. After checking the MF prices and estimating a reasonable sale price in our head we should quickly make sure that our price will make sense with what FBA competition we have. Our copy should be price at more than $12.90 but less than $24.40.

So, our estimated sale price for this book would be $16.70 + $3 (FBA up charge) = $19.70, which is less than $24.40 (New FBA) but more than $12.90 (Used Good FBA)

Since $19.70 exceeds our criteria, we'll move on.

Determining Rank

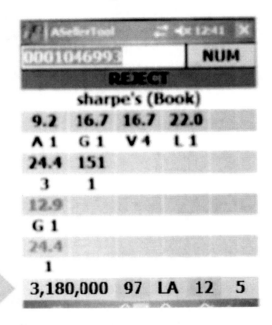

The Amazon Sales rank of this book is found at the bottom to the layout and is 3,180,000. Since this sales rank is less than our 5,000,000 max, we can move on to the next step. For more information about sales rank and when you may want to buy books with a rank higher than 5,000,000 go back to the book buying criteria section.

Quick Condition Assessment

If price and rank meet the buying criteria there's only one more thing you need to consider, is the book and all of its promised extras included. According to Amazon's Terms and Conditions we cannot sell incomplete books. If it's a workbook, it must have all of its pages intact. None of them can be missing. If it promises a Disc of some sort, the disk must be included.

If there is markings and highlighting it cannot completely mare the text. Every single page needs to be readable or it cannot be sold.

There are some types of books that Amazon doesn't allow us to sell, these include; Instructors/Teachers Editions or International Editions (for textbooks). Be sure to steer clear of those.

Conclusion

That's essentially it! If you can practice using the PDA for a while and familiarize yourself with the buying criteria reading the layout, making quick decisions will seem like a natural process to you. In fact, after a little training you should be able to scan books on a shelf at a rate of about 1 per 2 seconds, all things considered.

Sourcing Locations

You're armed with the tools and the determination to use them, now what? Where do you go to find books? The good news is that there are typically more sourcing locations in your area than you probably think. I am going to go through all of them, one-by-one so that you can 1) understand the book sourcing landscape, and 2) hopefully give you some tools that will help you succeed sourcing books.

Make a Map

Before you hit the streets I recommend that you put together a map. Whether you will be searching in retail stores, sales calls or thrift stores, save yourself a considerable amount time by doing some research beforehand. Using Google Maps and a tool that came pre-loaded on most Windows computers called a Snipping Tool, you can create a full color, detailed map with all the important locations marked and numbered. On the reverse side of the map, I suggest that you print out a numbered list of all of the stores with addresses so that while you are traveling around town you'll have some direction. This way you can familiarize yourself with the geography, the roads, towns, etc., or simply plug the addresses into the GPS on your phone.

Also, when you map out stores for, make sure to string them along, in the order of highest efficiency. If you are planning on spending the day sourcing around in a metro area, you should definitely approach it systematically. Save yourself some time and energy and try to hit the stores in order, say from East to West, as much as possible. Also, if you're going to drive downtown make sure that you determine a route to avoid any rush hour traffic at all costs. There's no need to have you pushing through stop and go traffic if it can be avoided.

What Types of Books Should be Scanned?

If you ask 10 different booksellers, you may get 10 different answers. But usually, we are all in agreement that non-fiction is the best overall category to source books in. These are my favorite book categories in order:

1. Reference (textbooks)
2. Business
3. History
4. Biography
5. Religion
6. Arts and Crafts
7. Health
8. Travel

I encourage you to hit each of these sections in this order. But, if you want to venture into other sections, you are more than welcome to. In fact, we just sold a handful of Children's books, although we usually don't have much luck in that section.

Next, we are going to talk about strategy and about the places that I think are best for Book-sourcing:

1. Thrift-Stores

Thrift stores are our most reliable source of inventory. They are far more predictable and regular than the other options. If you know how to work the sales, they can also offer books at or below the $2 minimum purchase price, which is what you will be on the lookout for. I'll get into library book sales in a bit, but one advantage to thrift stores, over library sales is that if you go during the week and during the day, you won't have to fight crowds. I'm an introvert. I would much rather scan books without people looking over my shoulder or getting in my way. If your shoppers are wired the same way, they will appreciate the less competitive nature of a thrift store.

Which Thrift Stores?

Okay, so I talked you into putting together a map and that's great. But, which stores and locations are you going to put on it? You know you need to send them somewhere, but where? We create a map for each different thrift-store chain in your area. So, we have a map of all of the metro area Goodwill stores, a map of all the area Savers and Unique stores, a map of all of the Salvation Army Thrift stores, a map of all of the Value-villages, and a "best of the rest" store map. If you haven't already, you should really familiarize yourself with what sourcing opportunities are in your area, and then type them up and print them out. Google search "Thrift Store" and drive around town. Some thrift stores don't have a website, and/or they haven't positioned themselves online very well and it would be hard to find them by searching Google. Don't leave any stone unturned!

Typically, people who have worked "normal" jobs their whole life may find it difficult, at first, to do more than you ask of them. Someone who has been an exchangeable cog in someone's factory or business their whole life is used to their bosses telling them exactly what they need to do. Thinking for themselves and thinking outside of the box is often discouraged. I was there once, I know! So, at least in the beginning, spoon-feed them as much as you can. Set them up for success, and make it so that they don't have to do much thinking. Once you have invested in them, and enriched their minds to the possibilities that are out there, then you can encourage them to branch out and find opportunities that you haven't discovered yourself.

Document Reoccurring Thrift Store Sale Days

Next, we need to figure out when to send them to these stores. Familiarize yourself with the various reoccurring sales and discounts that your list of stores offer throughout the week. The book prices at some of our local Goodwill stores can be frustratingly high, but did you know that on certain days of the week they discount certain tag colors? Why not have your shoppers hit the stores on these days and specifically look for these colored tags? Your only opportunity to gather up inventory that meets your criteria may be on these sale days.

Also, many thrift-stores offer discounts for people who donate. At Savers (a thrift-store in the mid-west) they give you a 20% off coupon when you donate two bags or more, and this coupon can be used towards inventory. Sticking with Savers, all stores have an offer "Buy 4 books, Get 1 Free". When we take advantage of this deal coupled with a freshly earned 20% off coupon, we're well on the way to helping our shoppers hit their $2 per book maximum buying price.

Call or visit all of the stores in your area and write down which days they have sales and what kind of discounts your shoppers can expect. Beyond the weekly sales and discounts that they offer, ask them for the details of any other sales that they have throughout the year, such as Presidents Day and Martin Luther King Jr. Day. It may be a good idea to put these in on a monthly calendar to give to your Book-Sourcing team.

Talk to Management

Books can be a thrift store's worse nightmare. A typical store will have shelves and shelves of books on the sales floor but may also have an equal amount or more books in the back waiting to be shelved. Our local store has to move the entire book section, across the store, several times a year! Usually the books are displayed up front but for Halloween and Christmas they are relocated to the back of the store. Don't you think that these thrift store managers want these books to sell? You may be their only opportunity to unload all of their pretty obscure titles.

I would highly recommend that you schedule a brief appointment with the store manager to see if they would be willing to give you a discount for making a bulk purchase. If you're not sure what to say, say something along the lines of, "I'm planning on buying over 100 books today and I was wondering if you would be willing to offer me an additional discount for buying such a large amount?" They may only offer you an additional 10-20% off, but it's worth it right?

Andrew, our book-selling manager, asked this very question to the manager of a small Christian books store in the cities and he was quickly ushered into the backroom. The manager said that they have more books than they had room out front and that he was welcome to scan the shelves in the back. He was also extended an additional 20% off, which is fantastic!

Don't Thrift Stores Sell Books Online Now?

This objection to thrift-store sourcing comes up from time to time and it's worth considering. There are some Goodwill stores that scan books in the back and then pick the good ones out to be sold online. Although this isn't good news for us online book-sellers, don't let it discourage you too much. This is why, Goodwill sells books on Amazon and Merchant Fulfills them. This means that books that would be a profitable FBA selection, but not a good MF sell, will be overlooked.

Time and time again, we scan a book that is selling Merchant Fulfilled for only a couple of dollars plus shipping ($3.99). This would cost the customer $5.99 and would probably be a book that the thrift-store would skip. But, that same book could be sold by a Fulfillment by Amazon seller, in the same condition, for $10.95+. For $5.99, the Amazon customer would get the book that they wanted in the condition that they wanted from this third-party seller (MF). But they would have no guarantee of when it would arrive and they would have the added anxiety of knowing that they would have to deal with this little, possibly stubborn book-seller, if things went wrong. The allure of having guaranteed 2-day shipping plus the promise of being able to work with Amazon directly if returns need to be made often motivate people to spend extra money on a book that is Prime Eligible (or FBA) rather than buying a much cheaper book that's Merchant Fulfilled.

I once sold a book for $24.95 FBA, and the very same book in the very same condition was being sold MF for only $8.95. This means that the customer valued the expedited shipping and the promise to work with Amazon directly, if there was a problem, so much that they were willing to pay over $15 more for the same book! This is not an irregular occurrence.

2. Book Sales

Library sales are a great place to find cheap books. Depending on which sales you go to, they can be a bit crowded. But if you don't mind navigating your way through the narrow aisles of a sale, then you will be very pleased. On average, the books sourced at library sales are acquired for less than a dollar, and if you hit a library sale on their last day often times you can buy books at less than fifty cents apiece. This is much cheaper than the prices that most thrift stores have to offer. Also, the sheer volume of books that you can source can make even your best thrift store look pathetic.

When it comes to library sales, and other large book sales, there are national and local sales that you should be on the lookout for:

National Sales

If you haven't already, you should swing over to www.booksalefinder.com to check out their list of national book sale events that are taking place this year. Just like any other book source, there are pros and cons to national book sale events.

The Pros: National sales events usually sell a ton of books. One year, we traveled to St. Louis to attend the million+ book YMCA sale, and the amount of books that they had was insane. I literally had to spend two full days of scanning just to be able to get through all of the non-fiction sections. We sourced over 700 books on that trip, and we prepped and shipped them out of the hotel room the next day, which was pretty sweet!

ProfitSourcing.com
Every major city seems to have book sales published on this site.

The Cons: There are draw-backs to these heavily advertised national sales events. Every other book seller in the country knows that they exist and if the sale is big enough, it will likely garner the attention of book sellers across the nation. At the YMCA sale, I arrived at the sale at 5am in the morning to wait in line. The doors opened at 9am and we arrived early in order to be given a ticket that held our place in line for the sale, which started in the afternoon. Suffice to say, I was number 42. Everyone in front of me and the hundred or so people behind me were all book sellers, with scanners in hand, ready to hit the stacks. It was actually pretty exciting, even though I would rather source for books without all of the buzz.

I'm not trying to spoil national sales for you, I just want to give you a heads up to the seriousness some other sellers take these events. I was standing in line with a couple of gals from Colorado, at another national sale, and we got to talking. They sold children's books on eBay, and the lady in front of me sold antique books. Neither of them were looking for the same books that I was be looking for. Even if there were some other Amazon sellers there, are they selling FBA? What is their minimum allowable sales price? Are they lazy scanners? Do they skip books that don't look good?

There is a local book seller (he owns his own Amazon selling business) here in my home town whom I know well. He only buys books that he can sell for at least $25 and they have to have rank of less than 1,000,000. Typically, he would go to a store that would net us over a hundred books on a bi-weekly basis but he would only find 4 or 5. His criteria, in my opinion, is way too stringent. He's leaving way to many books on the shelf. Also, the amount of time that he's spending to find only 4 or 5 books would be maddening to me.

Local Sales

Book sales that tout 100,000 books or less tend to be ignored by the hordes of book-sellers, and these are usually the best! Some of these sales are advertised on the BookSaleFinder.com website, but others you'll have to do some digging to find. Start contacting local libraries, with a pen and paper handy. Ask them when they have sales, how much they charge (to get in and per book), whether or not they have a preview night and if they allow "scanners".

For local sales we try to go to the preview night, if there is one, and then also on the last day. Most library sales finish off with a Bag Sale Day. For some of our sales, that means that each bag full of books only costs $5, instead of the typical $1-2 per copy. Our local libraries organize by county, so 4 or 5 locations will collaborate and have a sale together at one location quarterly or bi-annually. It's good to put in the work to find these sort of things out.

What is a "Preview Night"?

Most book sales will open their doors early for their book buying customers that would like to shop before the doors officially open the following day. If it's a Friends of the Library run sale, there is usually a fee that must be paid at the door prior to admittance. Also, these special sale events only last an hour or two. The benefits of going to the preview sale is that you will have first crack at the books before it is open to the general public. If there is any competition in town, you'll be able to at least have a fighting chance at the good books! I recommend that you go to both the preview night and the bag sale at the end of the week. It's good to take advantage of both of these opportunities.

What does it mean if a Sale Doesn't Allow "Scanners"?

Some sales that you find online will say something like "no scanners allowed" in the fine print. What does this mean? Great question! Unfortunately there are some bad apples out there that have given book-scanners a bad name. In the name of finding the most amount of profitable books as fast as possible, they tear up a book sale which completely ruins the sale for those who are organizing it and those who are attending it. I have heard stories of people with scanners grabbing books out of their sections by the handfuls huddling with them in corners, to scan through them quickly, only to leave the discarded books in a pile somewhere. Other, rude book-scanners have thrown blankets or tarps over entire sections to prevent other shoppers from looking at those books until they have had the time to scan through them. This behavior is discouraged by book sale operators, and it should be!

Unfortunately, some of these sales have come to the conclusion that the only way to eliminate this sort of behavior is to ban all "scanners". If you've found a sale that states "no scanners" give them a call or stop by and plead your case. Tell them that you will be very respectful of the other shoppers around you and that you promise to leave the books tables in better condition than you found them. They may make an exception! When training our book sourcing team, we encourage them to be the most courteous shopper the book section has ever seen. It makes for a good business relationship with the store of the sale workers if you clean and organize as you go. It's these little things that can assist you in forming some lucrative partnerships.

3. Other Places to Find Books

While it's true that the first two sources for books account for the bulk majority of our inventory, there are other sources to consider.

Estate Sales

There are several estate sale websites that may be worth you time to sift through occasionally. If the sale advertises a large number of non-fiction books for sale, it may be worth checking out. Be sure to call the company that is having the sale and ask them 1) How many books the sale will have 2) How much they will cost per title and, 3) Would they be willing to give you a discount if you bought a very large number of their books?

Garage, Yard and Rummage Sales

Garage, yard and rummage sales can be great places to find books. Just like with estate sales, it's important to check beforehand if they have any books for sale and what they plan on charging per title. Garage and yard sales typically have the cheapest books but sometimes the selection lacks. It's good to plan ahead. Does your town have a city-wide garage sale day in the summer? It would be much easier to go quickly, from house to house scouting for books than it would be to drive all around town to hit up only a couple of sales. Again, efficiency is the key.

Craigslist Ads

Another excellent place in which you can find books is Craigslist. This can be done by either looking for books that other people are selling, or by advertising that you are interested in buying, and therefore having the books come to you. Just put together a concise criteria for the books that you're looking for and what you are willing to pay, otherwise you may get some interesting calls from people who are eager to offload their entire Romance collection!

Recycle Centers

Books that are on their last leg are shipped off to a recycle center for disposal. Generally, books need to be de-bound before the paper can be recycled due to the glue in the binding. You should contact your local recycling center and ask them if they ever get books in that they have no idea what to do with. You may be able to score some free inventory!

Paying For the Books

Once the books have been sourced you'll need to pay for them. Although this can be accomplished in a number of ways we feel like one way in particular is the best way.

You Buy the Books On Your Credit Card

We think that the best way to pay for the inventory is to have you buy it on your credit card and then we will reimburse you for it every other week. One of the reasons why we feel like this is the best option is because as an independent contractor (more on this later) you will be essentially running your own business. It would make sense for you to buy the books and for us to reimburse you for them. Here are some of the Pros and Cons worth considering.

The Pros:
- You'll be able to take advantage of all the Credit Card rewards for the book purchases. Whether that's cash-back or frequent flier miles you directly benefit from using the credit card. We recommend the Chase Visa Signature card and/or the Spirit Airlines MasterCard, but there are so many options.
- We will ensure that your credit card is paid off in full every month (as long as they are charges directly related to the business). This means that you don't have to worry about negatively affecting your credit, in fact quite the opposite.
- Your credit as an individual will grow as a result of using a credit card in this way which could prove to be very helpful for you down the road.

The Cons:

- You will assume all of the liability for these purchases until you are reimbursed. Since you will be paid every other week this won't be a problem, but it's worth mentioning.
- If you have a problem abusing credit cards, this opportunity to spend money that you don't have, using your new business card, may be more temptation than you can bare. If you feel like you are going to struggle with this let us know and we can discuss some strategies that we can employ to help you overcome this temptation.

Other Payment Options

If for whatever reason you can't or don't want to use your own credit card for the purchase of the books we'd be happy to discuss with you the other payment options.

Time to Hit the Shelves!

Now that you've acquired a barcode scanner, established your buying criteria and have spent some time finding and researching local thrift-stores & book sales, I recommend that you get out there and do some scanning yourself! Book scanning can be lots of fun. You work your way down the shelves searching for profitable books, and when you finally do discover one it's quite the rush. Some people think that sourcing is sort of like looking for treasure. Imagine you're a pirate looking for gold!

The thought that gets me most excited is thinking about all of those profitable books that are just sitting there on a thrift-store or library sale book shelf, waiting to be sourced and re-sold. Before, it was impossible to determine, at a reasonable pace, whether or not a book is worth reselling, but now with technology this can be determined very quickly.

Don't Over Look the Value that You Provide in this Business

Often times books in this environment, are on their last legs. If they hit the library sale or thrift-store and they still can't find a new permanent home, then unfortunately they will more than likely end up in a landfill. Books are very difficult to recycle due to the glue on the binding, so unless your local recycle center has a book de-binder, which most don't, off to the garbage they go. Many of the books that we source are hard-to-find, out-of-print books, and this is why people are happy to pay well over MSRP for them. Think about it. Our wonderful Amazon customers are looking high and low for a particular book but they can't find it anywhere. When they look up the listing on Amazon, they are pleased to discover that we, a 3rd party merchant, are selling a gently used copy of the book that their dying to get.

We have the privilege of doing the hard work of sourcing, prepping and shipping these books into Amazon so that they can be listed for grateful customers to buy. We book sellers provide a great service. We take books that are seemingly destined for destruction, rescue them and put them in the hands of someone who wants them. Not only is book selling great for the environment, but it's good business!

ProfitSourcing.com

Compensation

How You Will Be Paid

After considering all compensatory options we have decided that they best way to pay our Book Sourcers is on a per book finder's fee. It's pretty simple, for every book that you buy that meets our criteria we will pay you $1. So, them more books you source the more dollars you'll make.

What Does This Finder's Fee Translate to Per Hour?

Ultimately we value your time. We don't want you to have to trade dollars for hours when working for us. So if you are super productive in a short period of time that means that you can make great money, while freeing up your schedule to do what you want with it. Some Book Sourcers will work really hard at the beginning of the week so that they can take the rest of the week off.

We will do everything in our power to put you into a position to succeed. Meaning we will give you all of the training and tools necessary to help you make some excellent money sourcing books. That being said when you start out you can expect to reasonably make about $20-30/hour. This would mean that you would need to source 20-30 books within an hour, which is definitely doable, even for someone just starting out. As you get the hang of things you can expect the number of books sourced per hour to only increase.

A few weeks ago one of our Book Sourcers went to a library sale and bought 100 books in less than an hour, if you do the math, her hourly wage ends up being pretty fantastic!

When is Payday?

We will pay you every other Monday electronically. To help this process we will need your checking or savings account and routing number. We will pay you for all expenses directly related to the Book Sourcing business, the purchase price of all of the new inventory and your finder's fees.

On the Friday before payday we ask that you email copies of your receipts with a bi-weekly itemized tally of all of your expenses, the total cost of all of the books purchased and how many books total you sourced. You can take a picture of the receipt on your phone or you can scan a copy of it onto your scanner. Here's an example of the format that we would like you to send the information in:

Date	Store/Location	Cost	Books Sourced
06/02/15	Unique Thrift	104.39	66
06/02/15	Unique Thrift	93.37	67
06/06/15	Library Sale	25	29
06/09/15	Savers Thrift	106.57	66
Totals		329.33	228

Book Costs:	$329.33
Finders Fees:	$228.00
To Be Paid:	$557.33

Tallying everything up like we have in this example will help us process your compensation as efficiently as possible. Also be sure to include copies of your receipts like this:

Andrew 75

BURNSVILLE UNIQUE
14308 BURNHAVEN DRIVE
BURNSVILLE, MN 55306

06 08 2015   16:05:31
MID: 000000003578928   TID: 05447574
227084745990

Uni   CREDIT CARD

VISA SALE

650006
Discount
Coupon 1
13055
Net Price
650006
Discount
Coupon Nu
13055
Net Price
50006
Discount
Coupon Numt
13055

CARD #	XXXXXXXXXXXX0734
Chip Card:	Visa Credit
Chip Card AID:	A0000000031010
ATC:	0039
TC:	D7F4980CFC8ECA02
INVOICE	0041
Batch #:	000248
Approval Code:	008102
Entry Method:	Chip Read
Mode:	Issuer
Tax Amount:	$0.00

SALE AMOUNT $93.18

CUSTOMER COPY

A simple picture from your smart phone, attached to the email would be sufficient. If you have any questions about how to put together your bi-weekly compensation email, let us know, we'd be glad to help get you set up.

45

ProfitSourcing.com
Tips for Independent Contractors
Disclaimer – Be sure to consult a certified financial adviser or CPA

Unless told otherwise you will be considered an Independent Contractor. What this means is that you'll be responsible to calculate all income and expenses so that these things can be claimed at tax time next year. If you make more than $600 for the year we will be issuing you a 1099-MISC (which is required of us by law). This form will tell you, and the government, how much revenue that you've earned from us for the fiscal year. It will be your responsibility to report these earnings, offset by any expenses, on your tax return.

Essentially you'll be running your own Book Sourcing Business and we want to ensure that you are ready for it.

Make Sure to Document all Travel Expenses

As an independent contractor if you drive a car, van or truck to and from book sourcing locations be sure to track your mileage. Beginning January 1st, 2015 the standard deduction for mileage is 57.5 cents per mile. This means that you can take all of the miles that you've driven for business and multiply them by this standard rate and the government will allow you to deduct these on your tax return. These expenses will rightfully so offset some of your earnings for the year, and therefore what you're required to pay in for taxes (if you're required to pay). The IRS wants you to have an itemized list of all of your travel for the year.

I'd recommend that you grab a notebook and every time that you take a trip for business to document the date, number of miles traveled, destination, and the purpose for the trip. There are a handful of free and inexpensive phone apps that you can use to track mileage if you want to simplify things a bit. Regardless, you should definitely be taking advantage of this deduction it will save you a lot of money in the long run.

For more information about the IRS Standard Mileage Deduction do to this site: http://www.irs.gov/Tax-Professionals/Standard-Mileage-Rates

If you do any overnight traveling be sure to keep a record of food costs and hotel accommodations. A portion or all of these expenses could qualify for a tax deduction. If you'd like to learn more about which travel expenses are covered and which ones aren't, be sure to visit this site: http://www.irs.gov/taxtopics/tc511.html

Home Office Deductions

If you use a portion of your house to run this business you may be eligible for a tax deduction. You'll need to do some calculations at tax time but these deductions are definitely looking into. Basically, you determine how much you spend to maintain and run your household and then figure out what percentage of that overall space is used exclusively for this business and then you do some calculations to see what you're eligible for. Be sure to go to this link for more information: http://www.irs.gov/Businesses/Small-Businesses-&-Self-Employed/Home-Office-Deduction

All Other Expenses

Did you need to buy new equipment or supplies to run this book sourcing business? Be sure to document and keep receipts for everything, these purchases may be eligible for a tax deduction. http://www.irs.gov/uac/Deducting-Business-Supply-Expenses

Educational expenses such as, but not limited to attending conferences, purchasing books related to the industry of your business and other computer programs should be documented. Some of these expenses may be written off. http://www.irs.gov/Individuals/Qualified-Ed-Expenses

Conclusion

I would like to personally welcome you on to the team. I am confident that with the information that you've gleaned from this training manual and a little hard work on your part you'll be a great success. Book Sourcing is such an exciting business opportunity and I am confident that you'll not only make some great money but will also have tons of fun in the process! Happy Sourcing!

ProfitSourcing.com

Coming soon...

Book Flipping 2.0
The Online Course!

- Achieve Financial and Lifestyle Freedom
- 81 Training Videos
- 15+ Hours of Content
- 6 Training Modules in 6 Weeks
- Perfect for the New & Experienced Online Seller
- Real Entrepreneurial Strategies

To be notified as soon as registration is open sign up at:
https://profitsourcing.leadpages.co/thankyou/

ACKNOWLEDGMENTS

Thank you to everyone along the way that has given me the help and encouragement to make this book a reality.

First and foremost, I want to thank Chelsea, the love of my life. I couldn't accomplish anything in life without your support. When you believe in me and my ability to accomplish something, I feel like I can conquer the world.

A special thanks to my Mom and Dad, who have been a constant source of encouragement and support my entire life.

A big thanks and shout-out to all of the other people who have contributed to the making of this book;

George "the Pizza man" Thompson, you inspired this project from the beginning. Jeremy James, you're a constant source of feedback and encouragement, thank you brother. Melissa Voigt, thank you for helping me pick the right book-title. Chris Green, you helped in some "Big Ways" to get the ball rolling, thanks my friend. Andrew Voigt, you're killing it out there, thanks for helping make all of this success possible. Jonah VanProosdy, your hard work has opened up so much time for me to invest in coaching and spending time with my family. Thanks for being such a great friend and brother in Christ.

I don't have very many local entrepreneurial mentors, but I've been inspired by afar by; Jim Cockrum, Seth Godin, Gary Vaynerchuck, Robert Kiyosaki, Kevin Swanson, Malcolm Gladwell, Dale Carnegie, Robert Allen, Donald Trump, Dave Ramsey, Tim Ferris, Pat Flynn & Randy Alcorn.

The cover was designed by Alinda Velist, I found her on Fiverr.com, and was very pleased with her work (https://www.fiverr.com/alindavelist).

The book was edited by Daniel, also on Fiverr.com, and he did a great job.

Last, but definitely not least, I want to thank my Lord and Savior Jesus Christ. Without His saving grace in my life, some odd nine years ago, I would probably be dead. By grace through faith I was saved, and as a result given a new heart with new desires. Without this radical shift in my life I wouldn't be pursing the things that I'm pursing, helping others, and looking to maximize time with my family. Thank you God for blessing me and my family with this business and that clarity of mind which was essential to finishing this project. My prayer is that I can use what you have blessed me with to be a blessing to others. I pray that I can use this opportunity to glorify your name and further your Kingdom.

A big THANK YOU to all of my readers! Have a great day!

CPSIA information can be obtained
at www.ICGtesting.com
Printed in the USA
LVOW10s0929260617
539391LV00021B/704/P

9 781516 909667